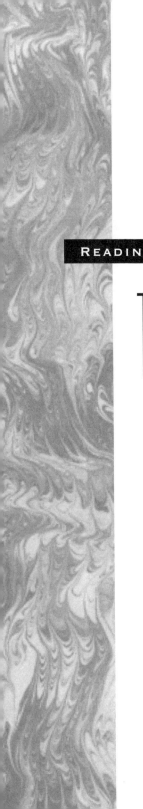

READINGS ON

THE SONNETS

THE GREENHAVEN PRESS
Literary Companion
TO BRITISH LITERATURE

THE SONNETS

David Bender, *Publisher*
Bruno Leone, *Executive Editor*
Scott Barbour, *Managing Editor*
Bonnie Szumski, *Series Editor*
Clarice Swisher, *Book Editor*

Greenhaven Press, San Diego, CA

Library of Congress Cataloging-in-Publication Data

Readings on the sonnets of William Shakespeare / Clarice
   Swisher, book editor.
         p.   cm. — (Greenhaven Press literary companion
   to British literature)
      Includes bibliographical references and index.
      ISBN 1-56510-571-0 (pbk. : alk. paper). —
   ISBN 1-56510-572-9 (lib. bdg. : alk. paper)
      1. Shakespeare, William, 1564–1616. Sonnets.
   2. Sonnets, English—History and criticism. I. Swisher,
   Clarice, 1933– . II. Series.
   PR2848.R38   1997
   821'.3–dc20
                                                    96-23046
                                                        CIP

Cover photo: © Corbis-Bettmann

Copyright ©1997 by Greenhaven Press, Inc.
PO Box 289009
San Diego, CA 92198-9009
Printed in the U.S.A.

> **"Two loves I have, of comfort and despair."**

**William Shakespeare
Sonnet 144**

CONTENTS

combined his powers of observation with his language facility to produce love lyrics that touch readers' most intimate feelings.

Chapter Two: Poetic Techniques Used in the Sonnets

Chapter Three: Themes in the Sonnets

Chapter Four: Analysis of Individual Sonnets

FOREWORD

> *"'Tis the good reader that*
> *makes the good book."*
>
> Ralph Waldo Emerson

The story's bare facts are simple: The captain, an old and scarred seafarer, walks with a peg leg made of whale ivory. He relentlessly drives his crew to hunt the world's oceans for the great white whale that crippled him. After a long search, the ship encounters the whale and a fierce battle ensues. Finally the captain drives his harpoon into the whale, but the harpoon line catches the captain about the neck and drags him to his death.

A simple story, a straightforward plot—yet, since the 1851 publication of Herman Melville's *Moby-Dick*, readers and critics have found many meanings in the struggle between Captain Ahab and the whale. To some, the novel is a cautionary tale that depicts how Ahab's obsession with revenge leads to his insanity and death. Others believe that the whale represents the unknowable secrets of the universe and that Ahab is a tragic hero who dares to challenge fate by attempting to discover this knowledge. Perhaps Melville intended Ahab as a criticism of Americans' tendency to become involved in well-intentioned but irrational causes. Or did Melville model Ahab after himself, letting his fictional character express his anger at what he perceived as a cruel and distant god?

Although literary critics disagree over the meaning of *Moby-Dick*, readers do not need to choose one particular interpretation in order to gain an understanding of Melville's novel. Instead, by examining various analyses, they can gain numerous insights into the issues that lie under the surface of the basic plot. Studying the writings of literary critics can also aid readers in making their own assessments of *Moby-Dick* and other literary works and in developing analytical thinking skills.

The Greenhaven Literary Companion Series was created with these goals in mind. Designed for young adults, this unique anthology series provides an engaging and comprehensive introduction to literary analysis and criticism. The essays included in the Literary Companion Series are chosen for their accessibility to a young adult audience and are expertly edited in consideration of both the reading and comprehension levels of this audience. In addition, each essay is introduced by a concise summation that presents the contributing writer's main themes and insights. Every anthology in the Literary Companion Series contains a varied selection of critical essays that cover a wide time span and express diverse views. Wherever possible, primary sources are represented through excerpts from authors' notebooks, letters, and journals and through contemporary criticism.

Each title in the Literary Companion Series pays careful consideration to the historical context of the particular author or literary work. In-depth biographies and detailed chronologies reveal important aspects of authors' lives and emphasize the historical events and social milieu that influenced their writings. To facilitate further research, every anthology includes primary and secondary source bibliographies of articles and/or books selected for their suitability for young adults. These engaging features make the Greenhaven Literary Companion series ideal for introducing students to literary analysis in the classroom or as a library resource for young adults researching the world's great authors and literature.

Exceptional in its focus on young adults, the Greenhaven Literary Companion Series strives to present literary criticism in a compelling and accessible format. Every title in the series is intended to spark readers' interest in leading American and world authors, to help them broaden their understanding of literature, and to encourage them to formulate their own analyses of the literary works that they read. It is the editors' hope that young adult readers will find these anthologies to be true companions in their study of literature.

INTRODUCTION

Readings on the Sonnets offers students several kinds of information: a biography of William Shakespeare, critical essays on the sonnets, and a number of aids for using this book and for further research.

The critical essays selected for this literary companion provide teachers and students with a wide range of opinion about Shakespeare's sonnets. Critics try to identify the people about whom the sonnets are written. Because Shakespeare did not name his subjects or explain the circumstances that prompted the poems, scholars have tried for centuries to identify, plausibly if not conclusively, the beautiful youth and the dark lady and to determine whether or not the poems are autobiographical. Several essays discuss the general themes of the series or reveal the meaning of individual sonnets. Others analyze Shakespeare's poetic technique and offer opinions concerning its effectiveness. Still others report on the few among Shakespeare's contemporaries who mention the sonnets and speculate on the notable absence of criticism and commentary during his lifetime. This anthology gives students a cross section of the serious scholarship concerning Shakespeare's sonnet series. Numerous individual sonnets are quoted within the essays. Students preparing research papers or oral presentations will find in this collection abundant material from which to generate topics. Though this companion provides an excellent starting point, students will want to extend their research, perhaps by consulting the bibliography at the back of the book.

The essays have been written by scholars and critics from many different disciplines and time periods, from the 1880s to the 1990s. Both British and American authors are represented. Many of the authors are literature specialists and Shakespeare scholars; on the other hand, one is a publisher, one a freelance writer, one a poet, one a philosopher, and one a historian. Several of the most highly respected Shakespearean critics, including G.B. Harrison, J. Dover Wilson, Edward Dowden, G. Wilson Knight, and Stephen Booth, are contributors to this companion.

A number of special features make this anthology accessible and understandable. The annotated table of contents allows the reader to identify the subject matter of the essays at a glance. Introductions highlight the main arguments and point out key ideas covered in each essay; they also provide a thumbnail sketch of the author to let students judge the author's credibility. Within the essays, students will find subheads corresponding to the points identified in the introduction. Also within most essays, students will find relevant inserts taken from a variety of sources: Some quote from Shakespeare's sonnets, some offer an opposing viewpoint, some support the essay's argument, and some clarify terms.

A concise chronology following the essays lists the most significant events in Shakespeare's life and in England during his lifetime. A list of Shakespeare's works with dates follows the chronology. Because Shakespeare left no dated record of his works, some controversy exists among scholars as to the real chronology of Shakespeare's work. The dates for this list of works are based on the conclusions drawn by scholar and critic G.B. Harrison. Because analysis of poetry involves technical terms, a glossary defines terms used by the authors of these critical essays. A bibliography for further research includes sources for historical background and critical commentary for the most part not covered in this anthology. Together, these aids for students make the task of research manageable and satisfying.

WILLIAM SHAKESPEARE: A BIOGRAPHY

By today's standards, factual information about William Shakespeare is meager indeed; no diaries, journals, or letters survive to help biographers ascertain the author's personality or his opinions or beliefs. By Elizabethan standards, however, more records exist concerning the events in Shakespeare's life than one would expect for most untitled persons. Diligent scholars have located institutional records to identify Shakespeare's place of birth and upbringing and the essential events in his family life. They have unearthed records identifying some of his employment history and economic holdings. To supplement the record, scholars have turned to the text of his works and knowledge of Elizabethan history and beliefs to understand Shakespeare the man. Not surprisingly, interpretations differ.

BIRTH AND FAMILY

William Shakespeare was born in Stratford (today called Stratford-on-Avon) in Warwickshire, a county in the heart of England, on April 23 or 24, 1564. His birth date is presumed from the record of his baptism in Holy Trinity, the Stratford Church of England, on April 26; because so many children in that era died in infancy, baptism usually occurred within two or three days of a child's birth. Shakespeare's mother, Mary Arden, came from an old county family. More genteel and prosperous than the Shakespeares, the Ardens provided their daughter with a dowry of land and money, which advanced the status of her husband, John Shakespeare, when the couple married in 1557. John Shakespeare was a wool dealer and glove maker in Stratford and, for a time, a prominent community leader and officeholder. He began public service as the town ale taster in 1557, and subsequently performed the offices of burgess, constable, town treasurer, alderman, and bailiff, or mayor. In the early 1580s, however,

John Shakespeare's financial troubles led to the loss of both his wealth and his governing positions.

William was the third of eight children born to Mary and John Shakespeare. Two daughters, Joan, christened in September 1558, and Margaret, christened in December 1562, died young. Four siblings born after William reached adulthood: Gilbert, christened in October 1566; a second Joan, christened in 1569; Richard, christened in March 1573 or 1574; and Edmund, christened in 1580. Another daughter, Anne, died at age eight.

EDUCATION

Though no school records exist, William likely attended public schools like the ones children throughout England attended. Typically, young children first spent a year in an elementary school for their letters (alphabet), numbers, and catechism (a summary of the basic principles of Christianity in question-and-answer form). After age seven, he probably attended grammar school at King's New School, where he received a rigorous education in classrooms taught by Oxford University graduates. Simon Hunt and Thomas Jenkins, two of the headmasters during the years Shakespeare lived in Stratford, had advanced degrees.

Students were expected to be in their seats by 6:00 A.M. in the summer and 7:00 A.M. in the winter for a school day that began and ended with Bible readings, psalm singing, and prayers. Students memorized Latin grammar and studied logic, Latin composition, and literature. The curriculum included the Roman dramatists Seneca, Terence, and Plautus; Renaissance religious texts; the Roman poets Horace, Virgil, and Ovid; the complete works of Erasmus, the Dutch Renaissance scholar; and the works of Roman orators, philosophers, and historians. Shakespeare, who drew from Ovid's *Metamorphoses* for his own plays and poems, likely remembered the classic from his grammar-school days. According to scholar and critic George R. Price, in *Reading Shakespeare's Plays*, "This education was at least comparable with a modern college major in classics." Years later, contemporary English playwright Ben Jonson disparagingly called Shakespeare's learning "small Latin and less Greek," but, by Jonson's standards, "much" learning would have meant a five-year study of Latin, ending with a master's degree.

Shakespeare's education, however, extended well beyond

the Stratford grammar school. Elizabethan law required regular attendance in the Protestant Church of England, so Shakespeare would have grown up listening to readings from the Bible and the *Book of Common Prayer*, the liturgical book of the Church of England. Scholars have counted in Shakespeare's plays allusions to forty books of the Bible and many references to the commandments, quotations from the Psalms, and lines from the prayer book. In *Shakespeare the Man*, biographer A.L. Rowse calls Shakespeare a man educated in "the university of life." His plays display detailed knowledge of the entertainment, social mores, and culture of his native Warwickshire. Price says that we may

> be sure that the knowledge of hawking, hunting, and archery, of horses, dogs, and wild things, of peddlers, shepherds, and farm folk—this store of information in his plays and poems— was not acquired only from books, but indicates a normal freedom to roam the countryside and enjoy himself.

Though he lived far from London, Shakespeare had at least a few opportunities to experience some of its cultural riches while a boy in Stratford. When John Shakespeare was bailiff, probably in 1569, troupes of players began to perform in the Guild Hall in Stratford. Though there are no records of John Shakespeare's attendance, as bailiff he would surely have brought his family to the entertainments. Traveling actors continued to stage plays in Stratford every year from the time William was five years old. In 1575 Shakespeare had another taste of London life when Queen Elizabeth I visited the earl of Leicester at his castle at Kenilworth, a few miles from Stratford. Called a progress, the queen's entourage included courtiers on horseback, coaches, hundreds of servants, and numerous carts hauling supplies. Country crowds gathered to watch the procession and perhaps hear a word from the queen. During the queen's stay—for nearly a month—crowds surrounded the castle to enjoy the pageants, water shows, and fireworks displays produced in the queen's honor. Shakespeare's plays are filled with references to these and more facets of the education he received as a boy.

EARLY MANHOOD

Though no record confirms this, it is believed Shakespeare left school at about age sixteen. When Shakespeare was eighteen years old, he married Anne Hathaway, eight years older than he. Biographers have made much of the fact that banns for the marriage were called only once, on December 1, 1582, rather than the usual three times; the inference is that church officials hurried the marriage because Anne was already pregnant. However, because Elizabethans considered betrothal (engagement) a binding agreement and in some instances the same as marriage, her pregnancy was less unusual than modern customs might consider it.

After the marriage, the couple lived with Shakespeare's family on Henley Street in Stratford. On May 26, 1583, their daughter Susanna was baptized; twenty months later the young couple had twins, baptized Hamnet and Judith on February 2, 1585. How this twenty-one-year-old man supported his family is unknown. An antiquarian and gossip, John Aubrey, born a decade after Shakespeare died, collected facts and anecdotes about public persons. In his journal, he says that someone told him that Shakespeare taught school and worked in his father's butcher shop. Since John Shakespeare had no butcher shop, Shakespeare either worked in someone else's butcher shop or his father's leather shop. Among the myths surrounding Shakespeare's life is the story that he was caught poaching deer in a park belonging to Sir Thomas Lucy of Cherlecot, near Stratford. Historian Nicholas Rowe suggests that Shakespeare had to leave his business and family and take refuge in London to avoid prosecution, but the story has never been proved.

FIRST YEARS IN LONDON

The years 1585 to 1592 are called the "lost years" because no records of any kind document Shakespeare's movements or activities during the period. He probably went to London some time between 1585 and 1587, possibly joining up with a company of actors or striking out alone on foot. By one route, a man could walk to London in four days if he made twenty-five miles a day, lodging at inns along the way for a penny a night. In *Shakespeare: A Documentary Life*, Samuel Schoenbaum describes the city as Shakespeare would have found it on his arrival:

> The great city of contrasts spawned stately mansions and slum tenements, gardens and midden-heaped lanes. With the Court close to hand, it was the vital nerve-center for the professions, trade, and commerce, and the arts; London nourished the English Renaissance. Only in the metropolis could a playwright of genius forge a career for himself.

When Shakespeare came to London, attending plays was the most popular form of entertainment for all classes, from poor students to aristocrats. London boasted several theaters: The first, built in 1576 by James Burbage, was called simply the Theatre, and the Fortune, the Swan, and Blackfriars followed. Each theater had a resident company of actors performing plays and competing with all the other theaters for popular approval. During the twelve days of Christmas, the companies performed plays in Queen Elizabeth's court to entertain royal guests, and throughout the year traveling troupes drawn from the companies also performed in towns and cities outside London.

The story goes that Shakespeare began his career as a dramatist by holding horses outside the theater. More reliable information indicates that he acted in plays before he began writing them. Records show that Shakespeare had already written plays by 1592, some of which were performed before audiences. These early plays—*The Tragedy of Titus Andronicus*; *Henry VI, Parts I, II,* and *III*; *The Comedy of Errors*; and *Richard III*—mimic the forms laid out by the Roman playwrights he studied in grammar school. Though attending plays was popular London entertainment, many moralists complained that the jokes were too bawdy and that young men neglected their church duties in favor of playgoing. Consequently, society looked on actors as riffraff at worst and men of questionable reputation at best. Price comments: "When Shakespeare became an actor, he must have deeply grieved the heart of his father and mother, and he surely gave himself cause for extreme discomfort at times." John Aubrey mentions no misgivings, however, and writes: "He was a handsome, well-shap't man: very good company, and of a very readie and pleasant smoothe Witt."

Because Shakespeare was an outsider in London, a country man who lacked the sophistication and easy manners of the Cambridge and Oxford University men, he studied the ways of a gentleman, found a mentor, and read widely. Shakespeare looked to Cambridge-educated playwright Christopher Marlowe, who was the same age but who preceded Shakespeare in skillfully combining drama with poetry. In many plays throughout his career, Shakespeare pays tribute to Marlowe, though ultimately he eclipsed Marlowe as a dramatist. Shakespeare's romantic nature was influenced by the works of two English poets: Sir Philip Sidney's

sonnets and *The Arcadia,* a prose romance, and Edmund
Spenser's *The Faerie Queene,* an allegory glorifying England
and the queen. Shakespeare, who loved his country and her
history, also read the *Chronicles* of Raphael Holinshed, a historian who came to London early in Elizabeth's reign, and
the works of historian Edward Hall, who wrote about England's past royal families. Shakespeare borrowed from
these works for many of his plays and used poetic techniques like those of Sidney and Spenser.

With the early plays, Shakespeare had made his mark as
a playwright. In 1592 his reputation elicited a comment in a
journal left by Robert Greene, a popular Cambridge-educated playwright who died that year. In his *Groatsworth of
Wit,* Greene, complaining that the professional actors had
forsaken university men like him, specifically attacked
Shakespeare:

> Yes trust them not: for there is an upstart Crow, beautified with
> our feathers, that with his *Tygers hart wrapt in a Players hyde,*[1]
> supposes he is as well able to bombast out a blanke verse as
> the best of you: and beeing an absolute *Johannes fac totum,*[2] is
> in his owne conceit the onely Shake-scene in a countrey.

SHAKESPEARE AS A POET

About the time Greene's comment appeared, plague swept
through London, lasting through 1593, and the lord mayor
ordered the theaters closed. Shakespeare made his first attempt to publish poetry. He had wanted to be a poet, which
he considered a noble occupation; he thought acting and
writing plays were merely means to support his family.
None of his plays, which were written for live performance,
had been published by 1592. The printer Richard Field obtained license to publish Shakespeare's poems *Venus and
Adonis* on April 18, 1593, and *Lucrece* on May 9, 1594. Very
popular with the public, both went through several editions. Shakespeare's name was absent from the title pages
of both publications, but both included signed dedications
from Shakespeare to the earl of Southampton, Henry Wriothesley, who later became Shakespeare's patron. The earl
was twenty, wealthy, well educated, and the handsomest
man at the court of Queen Elizabeth. As a lover of art and
literature, he generously supported writers and supposedly

1. a play on Shakespeare's line from *Henry VI,* "O tiger's heart wrapt in a woman's
hide!"   2. a "John Do-Everything," a "jack-of-all-trades"

gave Shakespeare £1,000 when the theaters were closed. As a poet benefitting from the earl's patronage, Shakespeare dedicated twenty sonnets to the earl and wrote glowingly about him in many of the others.

For a brief six-year period, circulating sonnet series to attract the attention of important or wealthy patrons became a fashionable practice among Elizabethan poets. Poets competed to create the most elaborate imagery describing (usually) a beautiful woman and the intense suffering her rejection causes. In *A Life of William Shakespeare*, Sidney Lee explains Shakespeare's participation:

> Between 1591 and 1597 no aspirant to poetic fame in the country failed to court a patron's ears by a trial of skill on the popular poetic instrument, and Shakespeare, who habitually kept abreast of the currents of contemporary literary taste, applied himself to sonnetteering with all the force of his poetic genius when the fashion was at its height.

Shakespeare began writing sonnets in earnest in the spring of 1593 after he had secured the patronage of the earl of Southampton. He passed his unpublished poems in manuscript form to friends and other poets, but did not prepare them for publication.

Shakespeare wrote a series of 154 sonnets; some celebrate a beautiful young man and some express powerful passion for a mysterious dark lady at whose hands the poet suffers greatly. Since neither the young man nor the dark lady is named, critics have gone to great lengths to verify their identity. Most critics conclude that the twenty sonnets dedicated to the young man and the many others that celebrate him in glowing terms refer to the earl of Southampton. No less critical energy has been devoted to determining whether or not the sonnets are autobiographical. Biographer A.L. Rowse, who thinks they are autobiographical, identifies the young man as the earl of Southampton and the dark lady as Emilia Bassano, daughter of an Italian musician in the queen's court. Biographer Sidney Lee argues that identification is irrelevant and dismisses the idea that the sonnets express Shakespeare's own experience or feeling. He says, "Elizabethan sonnets of all degrees of merit were commonly the artificial products of the poet's fancy; . . . autobiographical confessions were not the stuff of which the Elizabethan sonnet was made." According to Lee, as a practiced dramatist accustomed to creating a variety of characters with all manner of feelings and experiences, Shakespeare was capable of the illusion of personal confession and employed it skillfully in the sonnets.

Moreover, Shakespeare, like other sonneteers, imitated and borrowed from other sonnets. He says in Sonnet 76: "So all my best is dressing old words new,/Spending again what is already spent." Shakespeare included sonnets in some of his plays and continued to write a few after their popularity peaked in 1593 and 1594. The last sonnet to appear in a play is the epilogue of *Henry V*, written in 1599, and one of the last known was Sonnet 107, written in 1603 on the event of Elizabeth I's death. Though not all of Shakespeare's sonnets are well crafted, critics praise the sweet, flowing lines of his best. A contemporary of Shakespeare's, Francis Meres, wrote in 1598 in *Palladis Tamia: Wit's Treasury*: "So the sweet witty soul of Ovid lives in mellifluous and honeytongued Shakespeare, witness his *Venus and Adonis*, his *Lucrece*, his sugared *Sonnets* among his private friends, etc."

THE TURNING POINT IN SHAKESPEARE'S CAREER

In 1594 Shakespeare's career turned away from sonnet writing. With the end of the plague, the earl of Southampton's patronage ended, and with the reopening of the theaters, Shakespeare established himself with an acting company. By the summer of 1594, a group of actors formerly with other companies had formed a company under the patronage of Henry Lord Hunsdon, lord chamberlain to the queen, calling themselves Lord Chamberlain's Men. They performed at various theaters—the Theatre, the Curtain, the Swan—most of which were clustered on the south bank of the Thames in the district of Southwark. Among the company's permanent members were Henry Condell, John Heminge, Shakespeare, Richard Burbage (son of the Theatre's builder, James Burbage), William Sly, and Will Kempe. Burbage, the famous tragedian, and Kempe, the famous comedian, played leading roles in plays Shakespeare wrote specifically for their talents. From then on, Shakespeare was completely involved in the theater: He wrote for the company, acted in the plays, and shared in the profits. While in London, he worked hard and played little; he lived during those years as a lodger in a quiet room near the playhouse where he could write without interruption.

Stratford remained the center of his personal life, however, the place to which he returned each summer and in which he invested his money. In 1596 and 1597 Shakespeare was occupied with three significant family matters. First in August 1596, Shakespeare's son Hamnet died; with the death of his eleven-year-old son, Shakespeare lost hope of perpetuating the family in his name. Anne Shakespeare was forty and could not be expected to have another child. Shakespeare expressed his grief in the play he was writing at the time, *King John*:

> Grief fills the room up of my absent child,
> Lies in his bed, walks up and down with me,
> Puts on his pretty looks, repeats his words,
> Remembers me of all his gracious parts,
> Stuffs out his vacant garments with his form.   (III, iv)

Secondly, though he had no son to carry on the family name, Shakespeare pressed to obtain the title and coat of arms of a gentleman, a status evidently important to him. So that he could be considered born the son of a gentleman, Shakespeare applied and paid cash for a grant in the name of his father. On October 20, 1596, Garter King of Arms William Dethick issued a coat of arms with a falcon and a silver spear and declared Shakespeare a gentleman by birth. Today, the coat of arms is displayed on the Shakespeare monument at Stratford. Then, in May 1597, Shakespeare purchased New Place, a large house in the center of Stratford with two barns and two orchards and gardens. Before he was thirty-five years old, Shakespeare had achieved the status of gentleman, property owner, and playwright, but he had lost his only male heir.

Shakespeare's first success as a playwright had come between 1593 and 1598. *The Taming of the Shrew* and *The Tragedy of Romeo and Juliet* exemplify the characteristics of his early plays; they include long explanatory speeches written in stiff verse and intricate plots that imitate Marlowe and the plays Shakespeare studied in grammar school. The style is characterized by elaborate imagery and an abundance of puns and wordplay. Yet, critics have called several of these plays lyrical, among them *Love's Labour's Lost* and *A Midsummer Night's Dream*, because they contain passages of beautiful description and passionate emotion. Besides comedy, Shakespeare also wrote history plays about England's past kings: *Richard II*, *Henry IV*, *Parts I* and *II*, *Henry V*, and *King John*. The plays about Henry IV and V were especially popular with audiences who loved the humorous character of Falstaff. During this period, Shakespeare also wrote *The Two Gentlemen from Verona, Much Ado About Nothing,* and *The Merchant of Venice.*

THE GLOBE THEATER

In 1597, James Burbage, who had built the Theatre in 1576, died and the Lord Chamberlain's Men lost their lease. About the same time, Puritans increased their opposition to what they perceived as the immorality of the city theaters. The Lord Chamberlain's Men found backing to buy and disman- tle the Theatre, move the boards across the Thames from London's city center, and build the Globe away from the Pu- ritans. By this time, Shakespeare had acquired enough wealth to buy a tenth share in the new playhouse.

The Globe theater outshone its competitors; it held two thousand spectators and was equipped with a bigger stage, a cellarage for graves and ghosts, a curtained space for intimate and surprise scenes, and a balcony. The audience was closer to the players, and the players had more flexibility to move quickly from scene to scene. In the prologue to *Henry V,* in which Shakespeare played the part of the chorus, he refers to the new theater with anticipation and humility:

> A kingdom for a stage, princes to act
> And monarchs to behold the swelling scene! . . .
>   Can this cockpit[3] hold
> The vasty fields of France? Or may we cram
> Within this wooden O[4] the very casques[5]
> That did affright the air at Agincourt?[6]

In the epilogue to *Henry V,* Shakespeare displays a char- acteristically humble attitude toward himself, writing:

> Thus far, with rough and all-unable pen,
> Our bending[7] author hath pursued the story,
> In little room[8] confining mighty men,
> Mangling by starts[9] the full course of their glory.

Though he himself may not have believed these words, he speaks as a gentleman throughout his works, self-deprecat- ingly calling himself "a worthless boat," "inferior far" to Marlowe. Others found this attitude charming, and Shake- speare soon gained a reputation for congeniality.

---

3. playhouse   4. playhouse   5. the actual helmets   6. the French village where Henry V defeated a larger French army   7. bowing   8. the theater   9. marring the story by telling it in fragments

The opening of the Globe marked a new phase in Shakespeare's reputation and art. Shakespeare's early work had established him as the leading dramatist in London; no one could touch him, though Ben Jonson wished he could. Aubrey reports Jonson's envy of Shakespeare: "He was wont to say that he never blotted out a line in his life. Sayd Ben Johnson, I wish he had blotted-out a thousand." Shakespeare's art was becoming more refined and subtle. Price says, "Art has replaced artifice. The style has become so fully expressive of the thought that audience and readers are unconscious of the poet's devices." Shakespeare, who was interested in the workings of human character, objectively displayed his characters' minds in their actions and speeches. The soliloquies of Brutus, Hamlet, and Iago, for example, lay bare not only their intentions but their very souls.

OUTPOURING OF COMEDIES AND TRAGEDIES

After 1598 Shakespeare's comedies and tragedies appeared quickly one after another. He turned from English history to Roman history and used *Lives*, by Greek philosopher and biographer Plutarch, as a source for plots. *The Tragedy of Julius Caesar*, dated 1599, explores Brutus's character and motives. Shakespeare also wrote three comedies to suit Will Kempe's acting: *The Merry Wives of Windsor*, in which Shakespeare revived the character of Falstaff; *As You Like It*, portraying many kinds of love; and *Twelfth Night*, a popular romance regarded as Shakespeare's most musical play.

After 1600 Shakespeare wrote his greatest tragedies, distinguished from the earlier works by more subtle language and deeper spirit. *Hamlet* and *Othello* came first. Shakespearean scholar and critic G.B. Harrison says that "*Hamlet* is in every way the most interesting play ever written"; for nearly four hundred years, it has challenged actors and scholars to interpret Hamlet's character. *Othello*, a unified and focused play, portrays evil in the character of Iago as he exploits Othello's jealousy and Desdemona's innocence to destroy them and their love.

Though Shakespeare continued to work, the period from 1598 to 1604 brought significant personal diversions. In September 1601 his father died in Stratford. The following May, Shakespeare bought 107 acres of farmland in Old Stratford for £320, and in September a cottage on Walkers Street. On March 24, 1603, Queen Elizabeth, who had actively sup-

ported the Lord Chamberlain's Men, died. James I succeeded her, took over the company, renamed it the King's
Men, and supported the players even more avidly than the
queen had, making them an official part of his court, dou-
bling their salaries, and increasing their annual court ap-
pearances from three to thirteen. In addition, he gave them
license to perform in any town or university. These changes
required Shakespeare to write for the approval of two audiences, the court and the Globe. Shakespeare's increase in income allowed him to invest £440 in tithes in parishes in
Stratford and surrounding towns, investments that brought
additional income of £60 a year.

THE KING'S MEN

From 1604 to 1608, as a member of the King's Men, Shakespeare's art changed again. He wrote two transitional comedies in which he experimented with new techniques to work
out dramatic problems. *All's Well That Ends Well,* an uneven
play seldom performed, involves a young woman who tricks
a man into becoming her husband. *Measure for Measure,*
called a problem play because the plot poorly fits the theme,
concerns a woman who compromises her chastity to save
her brother. G.B. Harrison calls it "one of Shakespeare's un-
pleasant plays"; other critics have spoken of it less charitably.

After 1604 Shakespeare's tragedies probed more deeply
into the minds of their heroes. *The Tragedy of King Lear* was
performed in King James's court during the Christmas holi-
days of 1606. Modern critics regard *Lear* as Shakespeare's
greatest play, though not his most popular. The play has a
double plot; Lear suffers at the hands of his daughters and
Gloucester at the hands of his son. Both die, but each has
one child who remains loyal. The play's greatness lies in the
psychological depth of Lear's character and the stark reality
of both human nature and nature's elements.

Shakespeare wrote *Macbeth* in 1606, as a tribute to James
I on the occasion of a state visit from the king of Denmark.
The play is set in Scotland, James's home before he became
king of England. The good character Banquo is a member of
the Scottish Stuart family, ancestors of James. Shakespeare
further honored the king, who was interested in witchcraft,
by incorporating three witches into the plot. Though he did
not find King James I an honorable man, Shakespeare ful-
filled his duty to the ruler upon whose patronage he de-

pended. Like *Lear*, *Macbeth* reaches below the rational level into the subconscious, where primitive experiences lie in recesses of the mind; the tragic Macbeth and Lady Macbeth having murdered King Duncan to put Macbeth on the throne, see their plot undone and suffer mental anguish before they too die.

After the four great tragedies, Shakespeare returned to Plutarch's *Lives* as a source for three more. *The Tragedy of Antony and Cleopatra* picks up the story of Roman history where *Julius Caesar* left off. *The Tragedy of Coriolanus* is a political play in which Shakespeare exposes the weakness of all manner of politicians and presents the crowd as a fickle mob in a tone more bitter than in his exposé of the crowd in *Julius Caesar*. *Timon of Athens*, an unfinished play, tells about an ancient Greek mentioned briefly in Plutarch's *Lives*.

During this period, when Shakespeare wrote one or more plays a year and kept a busy schedule of productions at court and at the Globe, little is known of his personal life. Only a few facts are known. His daughter Susanna married a well-known medical doctor from Stratford named John Hall on June 5, 1607. In September 1608 his mother, Mary Arden Shakespeare, died, and in October 1608 Shakespeare was named godfather to the son of Stratford alderman Henry Walker, whose son was named William in honor of Shakespeare.

In 1609 a respected publisher, Thomas Thorpe, published without Shakespeare's knowledge a book entitled *Shakespeare's Sonnets: Never Before Imprinted*. Since no copyright laws existed at the time, any person with a manuscript in hand could register it, publish it, and become its owner. Two factors indicate that Shakespeare had no part in the publication: The dedication appearing under the title was by the publisher, common practice when an author was not involved; and the volume contained numerous errors and even missing words, unlike the editions of the two poems that Shakespeare had prepared for printing. Thorpe loosely divided the sonnets into two groups—those addressed to a young man, 1–126, and those addressed to the dark lady, 127–154—but this division is hardly accurate. In the first group, only about 80 address a man; 40 could easily address a woman or a man; several are what biographer Lee calls "meditative soliloquies" not strictly addressed to anyone. After Thorpe's edition, the sonnets were not reprinted until

1640, and some critics think a displeased Shakespeare took measures to prevent further circulation in 1609.

THE FINAL PERIOD

After the outpouring of tragedies, Shakespeare's art changed again, in part because of changes in theater ownership and attendance. Blackfriars, a private theater owned by Richard Burbage, had been leased to a boys' company. Burbage, Shakespeare, and other actors bought back the lease and staged plays there for upper-class audiences more like those at the court of James I. Blackfriars audiences liked new plays, while the public audiences at the Globe preferred old favorites. This situation suited Shakespeare, who could, at Blackfriars, try new plays that were neither comedies nor tragedies. Some critics have called the new plays romances; others, tragi-comedies. These plays involve themes of re-union after long separation followed by reconciliation and forgiveness. The plots revolve around children lost and then found, divided parents brought together, or an innocent person threatened but rescued. Before characters find a haven, they have been through storms and stress, encountered evil, or endured suffering. Rowse says: "For all their happy end-ings, these plays have an atmosphere full of suggestion and symbol, suffused with tears."

Shakespeare wrote four plays in this new form. *Pericles* is a transitional play, written in two styles. Critics believe Acts I and II contain scenes written by another playwright, while Act III is by Shakespeare. After experimenting with *Pericles*, Shakespeare wrote *Cymbeline*, probably in 1610, a melo-drama about an innocent girl who flees mistreatment and encounters a host of crises before she is reunited with her repentant husband. *The Winter's Tale*, written in 1610 or 1611, is a moving tale of wrongs committed by one genera-tion and reconciled in the next.

The Tempest, a play written for James I to celebrate a court wedding, is Shakespeare's farewell to the theater. This fairy tale about a magician and his beautiful daughter ends with the reconciliation of two generations. In *Shakespeare: The Complete Works*, G.B. Harrison praises *The Tempest*:

> Shakespeare has finally achieved complete mastery over words in the blank-verse form. This power is shown through-out the play, but particularly in some of Prospero's great speeches, . . . or in his farewell to his art. There is in these

speeches a kind of organ note not hitherto heard. Shake-speare's thought was as deep as in his tragedies, but now he was able to express each thought with perfect meaning and its own proper harmony.

Prospero, the magician of *The Tempest*, recounts his tricks in words that some critics think apply aptly to Shakespeare. After cataloging the marvels he has conjured up over the years, from raging storms to corpses rising from the grave to a dimmed sun, he announces, "this rough magic / I here ab-jure, . . . I'll break my staff, / Bury it certain fathoms in the earth, / And . . . I'll drown my book."[10] Shakespeare's only play after this farewell was *Henry VIII*, a history full of pageantry, music, and ceremony.

Beginning in 1612 Shakespeare divided his time between Stratford and London and once went to Parliament to lobby for better roads between the two cities. In 1612 his brother Gilbert died, followed by his brother Richard the next year. Shakespeare spent 1614 and 1615 in Stratford enjoying his retirement and his daughters, but information about his wife, Anne, seems to be nonexistent. The parish register of Holy Trinity shows that on February 10, 1616, Shakespeare's younger daughter, Judith, was married to Thomas Quiney, the son of Shakespeare's old friend Richard Quiney. On March 25, 1616, while he was in fine health, Shakespeare made a will. He left a dowry and additional money to Judith and all lands and houses to his older daughter, Susanna, and her heirs. He left his wife to the care of his daughters and willed her the next-best bed, reasoning that Susanna and her husband needed the bigger, better one. To his sister he left money for clothes and the home on Henley Street. He gave small amounts of money to friends and money for rings to fellow actors of the King's Men. And he left money for the poor in Stratford. A month later, after a trip to London, he suddenly became ill and died on April 23, 1616, at the age of fifty-two. As he lay dying, the chapel bell knelled for the pass-ing of his soul, for the man for whom love was the center of the universe and the central subject of his many works.

During his lifetime, Shakespeare made no effort whatso-ever to publish any work other than the two long poems. His plays belonged to the members of the theater company, who sold individual plays for publication when readers requested

10. of magic spells

them in the early 1600s. In 1623—the year Anne Hathaway Shakespeare died—two actors from the King's Men, Henry Condell and John Heminge, collected Shakespeare's plays and published them in what is known as the First Folio, and they have been in print ever since. Some skeptics, doubting Shakespeare's genius, have speculated that his works were written by Francis Bacon or others. Such theories are advanced by the uninformed. As Price says: "No first-rate scholar has ever accepted the evidence offered by the Baconians or others who argue that Shakespeare did not write the dramas that his fellow-actors, Heminge and Condell, published as his."

CHAPTER 1

An Introduction to Shakespeare's Sonnets

READINGS ON
THE SONNETS

The Mysterious Q: The 1609 Edition of Shakespeare's Sonnets

Robert Giroux

Robert Giroux gives historical background on the book known as Q, the first volume of Shakespeare's sonnets, published in 1609. Only thirteen copies are known to have survived. After 1609, the book disappeared for a hundred years. Some critics think that the book was suppressed because Shakespeare apparently had circulated the sonnets privately but never intended them for public view. Q's many errors lead Giroux to conclude that Shakespeare must not have authorized its publication.

Robert Giroux, who calls himself an "amateur Shakespeare scholar," is an editor and book publisher of many eminent writers at his firm, Farrar, Straus and Giroux.

The book known as Q, from its quarto size, is one of the most famous, and mysterious, books in the history of publishing. This rare book, only thirteen copies of which are extant,[1] was published in 1609 in the paper-covered and unbound form usual for the period. It has eighty unnumbered pages. In the unlikely event that an unknown copy were to come on the market, it would fetch an astronomical price. The surviving copies differ slightly in overall dimensions, as a result of having been variously cropped before being cased in fine eighteenth- and nineteenth-century bindings.

Q contains not only the 2,155 lines of William Shakespeare's 154 sonnets (one of which has twelve, and another fifteen, lines, instead of the usual fourteen) but also his nar-

1. Six are in England (two at the British Library, two at the Bodleian, one at Trinity College, Cambridge, and one at The John Rylands Library, Manchester); six are in the United States (two at the Folger Shakespeare Library, two at the Huntington Library, one at Harvard, and one at the Elizabethan Club, Yale); and one is at the Bibliotheca Bodmeriana, Geneva.

Excerpted from *The Book Known as Q: A Consideration of Shakespeare's Sonnets* by Robert Giroux (New York: Atheneum, 1982). Copyright ©1982 by Robert Giroux. Used by permission of the author.

rative poem of 329 lines in forty-seven stanzas, entitled "A
Lover's Complaint." A few critics have refused to acknowledge this poem as Shakespeare's, including some who accept
the sonnets, yet its provenance[2] is exactly that of the sonnets.
The tides of Shakespearean scholarship can shift surprisingly: in 1930 the formidable scholar E.K. Chambers believed the authorship of "A Lover's Complaint" to be "open to
much doubt," while in 1960 George Rylands called it a "little-
appreciated Elizabethan masterpiece" by the author whose
name it bears in Q. Recent critics dispute not its Shakespearean authorship but its early or late dating; its relation
to a contemporary poem has become a focus of interest.

WILD SPECULATION

In a review of Robert Giroux's The Book Known as Q: A
Consideration of Shakespeare's Sonnets, *the* New York Times
*comments on the dearth of information about the origin of
the sonnets and resulting speculation as to the reason.*

For centuries the sonnets have puzzled and sustained both
general readers and scholars; indeed, the eminent E.K.
Chambers observed that "more folly has been written about
the sonnets than any other Shakespearean topic." There is
no such folly in *The Book Known as Q. . . .*
The "plot" [Giroux] proposes is simple. The poet is com-
missioned to write the first 17 sonnets, which urge a noble
young man to marry and have children. . . . Years pass; the
poet becomes known as a playwright. Much later the portfo-
lio of sonnets "falls into the hands of a publisher who prints
this work of an earlier era" without the poet's permission.
The result—"Q"—is met with a silence so total that the book
must have been suppressed soon after publication, either by
the poet or by his powerful friends.

In 1609 an author's "rights," as we know them, scarcely
existed. The licence required for publishing a book could be
obtained only by a member of the Stationers' Company, the
guild of printers. If a guild member gained possession of a
manuscript, and the wardens allowed it to be entered in the
register at the Stationers' Hall, he—not the author—became
the copyright owner. Q was entered for Thomas Thorpe on
20 May 1609 as "a Booke called Shakespeares *sonnettes.*"

2. origin or authenticity

THE SONNETS DISAPPEARED FOR ONE HUNDRED YEARS

The mystery begins: publication of the sonnets apparently met with total silence; there was no second edition of what unquestionably ranks with the greatest poetry in the language. On 19 June 1609 Edward Alleyn, the star of the Lord Admiral's Men, the actors who were the chief rivals to Shakespeare's company, recorded in his household accounts the purchase of Q for five pence; no other undisputed reference to the newly published book is known. It is astonishing that Q was never reprinted in Shakespeare's lifetime, in contrast to his two earlier books of verse, *Venus and Adonis* (1593) and *The Rape of Lucrece* (1594), both of which went into numerous editions.

A not widely known fact is that Q went underground for one hundred years. The sonnets did not reappear in their original form until 1711, when the London publisher Bernard Lintott, having obtained a copy of Q formerly in the possession of the playwright William Congreve, incorporated the 1609 text into a collection of Shakespeare's poems. The sonnets have never since been out of print.

Most of the sonnets had been used in corrupt and fraudulent form twenty-four years after Shakespeare's death in *Poems: Written by Will. Shakespeare, Gent.* This pirated volume was published in 1640 by John Benson, known chiefly as a printer of broadsides and ballads. He incorporated material from many sources—songs from the plays; the 1601 poem, "The Phoenix and the Turtle"; "A Lover's Complaint"; and everything else he could lay hands on, except *Venus* and *Lucrece*, which were protected by other publishers' copyrights. Apparently Benson saw his opportunity when Thomas Thorpe, the copyright owner of Q, died in 1639. Benson suppressed eight sonnets completely, and rearranged and bowdlerized[3] the rest, changing pronouns to make it appear that poems addressed to "him" were meant for "her." Nowhere does Benson use the word "sonnet": the verse form was thoroughly out of fashion by 1640. He transformed 146 sonnets into 72 new poems, running two, three, and even five sonnets together as if they were written as a single poem. He also invented 72 titles, like "A Bashful Lover," "Careless Neglect," and "Upon the Receipt of a Table-Book from His Mistress,"

---

3. modified by removing parts thought to be offensive

which readers took to be Shakespeare's. Benson added a preface falsely stating that the contents had been written in the last years of the poet's life and that, "himself then living," Shakespeare had vouched for the purity and authenticity of Benson's text. In addition, the book presents as Shakespeare's more than ten poems not written by him. Edward Capell, the eighteenth-century editor, called Benson's book "rubbish." If awards were given for rascality in publishing, John Benson would deserve a prize.

"There are *no* contemporary allusions to it [Q]." This statement by J.W. Mackail seems unbelievable, especially when one remembers the phrase about Shakespeare's "sugared sonnets," but it turns out that none of the allusions to the sonnets is an allusion to Q. In 1598 Francis Meres published *Palladis Tamia: Wits Treasury*, which described Shakespeare as one of "the most passionate among us to bewail and bemoan the perplexities of love." It included the informative and often quoted contemporary estimate of the poet: "The sweet witty soul of Ovid[4] lives in mellifluous and honey-tongued Shakespeare—witness his 'Venus and Adonis,' his 'Lucrece,' his sugared sonnets among his private friends, &c." This fascinating allusion to the sonnets in manuscript form, like the publication of two sonnets—"When my love swears that she is made of truth," and "Two loves I have, of comfort and despair"—in the 1599 anthology *A Passionate Pilgrim*, cannot be called references to Q, which they preceded by ten and eleven years, respectively. Edward Alleyn's notation of his purchase of Q in the summer of 1609, though indeed a contemporary allusion, was not discovered until 1881. . . .

WERE THE SONNETS SUPPRESSED?

The mysterious silence that greeted the appearance of Q went long unnoticed, and no one proposed a plausible explanation until 1922, when Frank Mathew suggested: "The neglect of the *Sonnets* of 1609 can only be explained by concluding that they were quickly suppressed." This was seconded in 1926 by J.M. Robertson: "[Q] is now a very rare book yet the natural presumption would be that in 1609, at the height of Shakespeare's contemporary fame, it would have found a considerable sale if it were not interfered with; and that a second printing would have followed in a few

4. Roman poet

years. . . . There is fair ground for a presumption that . . . [Q] was stopped.". . .

There is no direct evidence for the suppression of Q; it is all indirect, negative, and circumstantial, like the scarcity of surviving copies. But circumstantial evidence is evidence. If Q were not suppressed, it would be reasonable to suppose that the author might have had a hand in its publication. Is there any evidence of this? Shakespeare, who had turned forty-five the month prior to Thorpe's registration of the sonnets, and lived seven years more until his death in 1616, apparently had nothing to do with the production of Q, because, among other reasons, it was so badly proofread. This contrasts with the texts of *Venus* and *Lucrece*, both of which are impressively free of printing errors, carry his signed dedications, and apparently had careful reading, having been printed in London by Richard Field, his fellow-Stratfordian. Q, on the other hand, is riddled with errors.

MANY ERRORS IN Q

The worst, and perhaps most revealing, gaffe is the two pairs of parentheses, enclosing blank space, inserted on consecutive lines at the end of the twelve-line sonnet 126. It is an overcorrection, constituting a mistake, rather than an ordinary misprint. Someone other than the author (perhaps the publisher, Thorpe, or the printer, Eld) counted the lines, concluded that the couplet was missing, and decided to indicate its omission. He did not realize that the poem has a different rhyme scheme from the rest, or that the twelve lines function as a coda or *envoi* to the first series of sonnets. . . .

The most blatant printer's error—which stands out because each sonnet in Q begins with a large, bold-face initial capital—occurs in sonnet 122, in which the poet acknowledges a gift of blank-books or writing-tablets. In the opening line, the compositor doubled both the capital and comma: "*T* hy gift,, thy tables, are within my brain.". . .

The total number of errors in Q has been variously estimated, depending on differing views in matters of punctuation, at a minimum of fifty-three and a maximum of eighty-four, but the foregoing examples will suffice. They led the chief arbiter of Shakespeare problems, E.K. Chambers, to classify the text as "not a very good one. . . . There are sufficient misprints," he concluded, "to make it clear that the volume cannot have been 'overseen' . . . by Shakespeare."

Not overseen by Shakespeare, unauthorized for publication, probably suppressed, almost invisible for one hundred years—these interesting discoveries about Q provoke at least two questions: How *did* it get published? What was Shakespeare's reaction? One would suppose it to be much more difficult to answer the second question than the first, but when W.H. Auden touched on both matters in a BBC broadcast in 1964, he said he was sure he knew the answer to the second:

> How the sonnets came to be published—whether Shakespeare gave copies to some friend who then betrayed him, or whether some enemy stole them—we shall probably never know. *Of one thing I am certain* [italics mine]: Shakespeare must have been horrified when they were published.

What Is a Sonnet?

William Flint Thrall, Addison Hibbard,
and C. Hugh Holman

William Flint Thrall, Addison Hibbard, and C. Hugh
Holman explain the history, form, and variations of
the sonnet and define terms most frequently used by
critics in discussing sonnets. Developed in Italy in
the thirteenth century, the Italian, or Petrarchan,
sonnet is a two-part poem with no more than five
rhymes. English sonnet writers varied the form by
organizing the fourteen lines of the sonnet into three
units of four lines followed by a couplet. Thrall, Hibbard, and Holman also explain the relation of a sonnet's structure to its content.

C. Hugh Holman, who revised and enlarged the
original handbook of literary terms written by scholars William Flint Thrall and Addison Hibbard, taught
English at the University of North Carolina at Chapel
Hill. In addition, he wrote detective novels and literary criticism.

The two characteristic *sonnet* types are the Italian (Petrarchan) and the English (Shakespearean). The first, the Italian
form, is distinguished by its bipartite division into the OCTAVE
and the SESTET: the OCTAVE consisting of a first division of
eight lines riming *abba abba* and the SESTET, or second division, consisting of six lines riming *cde cde, cdc cdc,* or *cde
dce.* On this twofold division of the Italian sonnet Gayley
notes: "The octave bears the burden; a doubt, a problem, a
reflection, a query, an historical statement, a cry of indigna-
tion or desire, a vision of the ideal. The sestet eases the load,
resolves the problem or doubt, answers the query, solaces
the yearning, realizes the vision." Again it might be said that
the OCTAVE presents the narrative, states the proposition or
raises a question; the SESTET drives home the narrative by
making an abstract comment, applies the proposition, or

Excerpted from *A Handbook to Literature* by William Flint Thrall and Addison Hibbard, revised by C. Hugh Holman (New York: Odyssey Press, 1960). Reprinted with the
permission of the Estate of C. Hugh Holman.

solves the problem. So much for the strict interpretation of the Italian form; as a matter of fact English poets have varied these items greatly. The OCTAVE and SESTET division is not always kept; the RIME-SCHEME is often varied, but within limits—no Italian *sonnet* properly allowing more than five RIMES. IAMBIC PENTAMETER is essentially the METER, but here again certain poets have experimented with HEXAMETER and other METERS.

THE ENGLISH SONNET

The English (Shakespearean) *sonnet*, on the other hand, is so different from the Italian (though it grew from that form) as to permit of a separate classification. Instead of the OCTAVE and SESTET divisions, this *sonnet* type characteristically embodies four divisions: three QUATRAINS (each with a RIME pattern of its own) and a rimed COUPLET. Thus the typical RIME-

SONNET TERMS

This diagram of Sonnet 29 illustrates some of the most important terms critics use when discussing Shakespeare's sonnets.

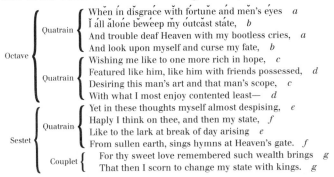

Quatrain: a 4-line unit
Couplet: sums up or comments on the previous 12 lines
Octave: states a problem or situation
Sestet: resolves the problem or illuminates the situation

Meter: the cadence, or rhythm, of a poem's lines
Iambic: the name of the sound unit that has one unaccented and one accented syllable. A sound unit is called a foot. An iambic foot is marked ˘ ´.
Pentameter: a measure of 5 sound units, or feet, per line. Note lines 1 and 2 have regular iambic pentameter.
Rhyme scheme: the pattern of rhymed end words

SCHEME for the English sonnet is *abab cdcd efef gg*. The COUPLET at the end is usually a commentary on the foregoing, an epigrammatic close. The Spenserian *sonnet* combines the Italian and the Shakespearean forms, using three QUATRAINS and a COUPLET but employing linking RIMES between the QUATRAINS, thus *abab bcbc cdcd ee*.

Certain qualities common to the *sonnet* as a type should be noted. Its definite restrictions as to form make it a challenge to the artistry of the poet and call for all the technical skill at the poet's command. The more or less set RIME patterns occurring regularly within the short space of fourteen lines afford a pleasant piquancy to the ear of the reader, and create truly musical effects. The rigidity of the form precludes a too great economy or too great prodigality of words. Emphasis is placed on exactness and perfection of expression. The brevity of the form favors concentrated expression of idea or passion.

The *sonnet* as a form developed in Italy probably in the thirteenth century. Petrarch, in the fourteenth century, raised the *sonnet* to its greatest Italian perfection and so gave it, for English readers, his own name. The form was introduced into England by Thomas Wyatt, who translated Petrarchan *sonnets* and left over thirty examples of his own in English. Surrey, an associate, shares with Wyatt the credit for introducing the form to England and is important as an early modifier of the Italian form. Gradually the Italian *sonnet* pattern (which had proved somewhat too rigid for English poets) was modified and since Shakespeare attained greatest fame for poems of this modified type his name has often been given to the English form.

The Origin and First Publication of Shakespeare's Sonnets

G.B. Harrison

In his introduction to Shakespeare's sonnets, G.B.
Harrison reports the few indisputable facts about the
first publication of the sonnets and provides background information about the brief popularity of
sonnet writing during the 1590s, a time when little is
known about Shakespeare's activities. Harrison also
summarizes the subject matter of the 154 sonnets in
series. The first 126 address a young man, the next
26 address a dark woman, and the last 2 are conventional love sonnets on Cupid. Critics have tried to
figure out whether the man and the woman are real
people (and, if so, who they are) or fictional. Harrison concludes that all critical commentary about
their identities is indeed speculative.

G.B. Harrison, a Shakespearean scholar who
taught in London and Canada before teaching at the
University of Michigan at Ann Arbor, edited a complete works of Shakespeare, wrote numerous critical
works on Shakespeare's poetry and plays, and published works about Elizabethan England, Shakespeare's time.

Shakespeare's sonnets are the most discussed and disputed
of all collections of poetry in the English language, and every
conceivable view has been expressed about them. Most critics, however, tend to join one of two parties. Some agree with
Wordsworth, who wrote:

> Scorn not the Sonnet; Critic, you have frowned,
> Mindless of its just honor; with this key
> Shakespeare unlocked his heart.

Others follow Matthew Arnold, who said:

Excerpted from *Shakespeare: The Complete Works*, edited by G.B. Harrison; ©1952 by
Harcourt Brace & Company and renewed in 1980 by G.B. Harrison. Reprinted by permission of the publisher.

> Others abide our question. Thou art free.
> We ask and ask—Thou smilest and art still,
> Out-topping knowledge.

These two observations sum up the main divisions between those who believe that Shakespeare was an inscrutable sphinx about whose personality we can know nothing and those who believe that Shakespeare has laid bare his heart in his plays and his sonnets.

There are indeed many lovers of poetry to whom all discussion of the personal and historical "problems" of the sonnets is distasteful, and who feel, not unreasonably, that such delicate works of art should not be dissected and anatomized. Such readers should leave these problems alone; indeed, theories about the sonnets are dreary unless the student studies the whole question for himself at first hand.

There are, however, certain indisputable facts. On May 20, 1609, Thomas Thorpe entered in the Stationers' Register[1] "a Booke called Shakespeares sonnettes." On June 19, Edward Alleyn,[2] in jotting down a list of purchases, noted "Shakspers Sonnets 5*d.*" The title printed on Thorpe's quarto reads:

SHAKE-SPEARES
SONNETS

Neuer before Imprinted.

AT LONDON
By *G. Eld for T. T.* and are
to be solde by *Iohn Wright,* dwelling
at Christ Church gate.
1609.

The volume is dedicated in a curious and enigmatic way:

TO . THE . ONLIE . BEGETTER . OF .
THESE . INSVING . SONNETS .
Mr W. H. ALL . HAPPINESSE .
AND . THAT . ETERNITIE .
PROMISED
BY .
OVR . EVER-LIVING . POET .
WISHETH .
THE . WELL-WISHING .
ADVENTVRER . IN .
SETTING .
FORTH .

T.T.

---

1. the company that authorized all matter to be printed for sale   2. an actor in the Lord Admiral's Company

By 1609 some of the sonnets were at least eleven years old. . . . In 1599, William Jaggard[3] had issued a little book called "*The Passionate Pilgrime. By W. Shakespeare.*" It contained twenty short poems, of which the first two were versions of Sonnets 138 and 144, and Nos. 3, 5, 17, poems taken from *Love's Labor's Lost.* The rest of the poems in the volume were by other authors.

THE STORY OF THE SONNETS

The volume of Shakespeare's *Sonnets* printed by Thorpe contains in all one hundred and fifty-four sonnets. As arranged in his edition, they tell a story of sorts. The first seventeen sonnets form a series. They are addressed to a beautiful youth and call on him to marry so that his type may be preserved and continued in his children. From Sonnet 18 to Sonnet 126, the poet addresses the youth on various topics and occasions and in a variety of moods. A sense of intimacy increases; admiration becomes love; but there is little method in the arrangement and no continuous story. The poet at first is shy and tongue-tied in the presence of his friend, and can only express himself in writing (23). The poet is separated from him by travel, but thinks continuously of the youth (27). He is outcast, but comforted by the thought of his love (29). He warns his friend not to honor him publicly, lest he become tainted with scandal (36). The friend steals the poet's mistress, but is forgiven (40–42). The poet has the youth's picture, which he wears at his breast on a journey (47–49). The poet is elderly (73). He is jealous because others seek the youth's patronage, especially one poet whose verse bears "proud full sail" (78–86). The poet gently rebukes the youth for wantonness (96). After a spring and a summer of separation the poet comes back to his friend (97–98). The poet congratulates the youth on his escape from a "confined doom" (107). He is reconciled after absence (109). He is disgusted with his profession (110–11). He defends himself against the charge of ingratitude (117). He apologizes for giving away the "tables" which the youth had given him (122). The last of this series is Sonnet 126.

Then follow twenty-six sonnets addressed to a dark woman, whom the poet has loved passionately but reluctantly. She is skillful in playing on the virginals,[4] faithless,

---

3. a London printer   4. small rectangular harpsichord without legs

wanton, physically unattractive, false to her husband, and yet irresistibly desirable. The collection ends with two conventional love sonnets on Cupid.

THE PROBLEMS OF THE SONNETS

There are thus a number of problems. If only we could answer any one of a dozen questions for certain, the enigma of the sonnets might be solved and our knowledge of Shakespeare greatly increased. The mysteries begin with the dedication. Even this has been interpreted in more than one way. Most assume that T.T. regards Mr. W.H. as the only begetter of the sonnets; but some read the dedication as implying that Mr. W.H. is wishing happiness to the only begetter.

Before considering these problems it is well to look at the probable date when Shakespeare's sonnets were written and at their place in Elizabethan poetry.

SONNETS DO NOT RECORD PERSONAL EVENTS

In Shakespeare's Sonnets, *Kenneth Muir writes that historical evidence, even if verified, still would not explain Shakespeare's Sonnets.*

Even though there were probably events in Shakespeare's life which resembled in some respects those treated in the Sonnets, we cannot assume that any of the poems records an actual event. Even if some future Hotson were to discover a number of affectionate letters written by Shakespeare to a noble lord, or a diary kept by his mistress, we should not be much nearer to establishing the literal, as opposed to the imaginative, truth of the Sonnets, though we might be able to add some pages to Shakespeare's documentary life.

The Elizabethan sonnet is the most famous of all verse forms, but its vogue was very short-lived. The sonnet form had first been introduced into English through Wyatt[5] and Surrey's[6] translations from Petrarch,[7] in the 1530's, and a few other English poets had written sonnets before 1590; but the popularity of the form was directly due to the publication of Sir Philip Sidney's[8] *Astrophel and Stella* in the spring of 1591. Anything written by Sidney was eagerly read, and this series of sonnets was at times so personal and sincere that it re-

5. poet and translator Sir Thomas   6. poet and translator Henry Howard   7. Italian poet and humanist   8. English poet

vealed to English poets possibilities hitherto unrealized. The most important collections of sonnets[9] ... all appeared within the next five years, and thereafter for several years sonnets were seldom published. It is most likely, therefore, that most of Shakespeare's sonnets were written during this vogue; that is, not before 1592 and probably not much after 1598. In style, they are akin rather to *Venus and Adonis* and some of the earlier plays. The greatest number of parallels of phrase and idea are to be found in *Love's Labor's Lost, Two Gentlemen of Verona, Romeo and Juliet, Venus and Adonis, Lucrece, Richard the Second* and *Richard the Third*, all of which were written by 1595. Moreover, if the sonnets stand in approximately the order of their writing, it seems clear from Sonnet 104 that they cover a period of more than three years. . . .

As for the fair youth, there are at present two main choices, Henry Wriothesley, Earl of Southampton, and William Herbert, Earl of Pembroke. Southampton was born on October 6, 1573 and succeeded to the title at the age of seven. He was therefore a ward (i.e., a minor needing a guardian) until he came of age. Lord Burleigh, Queen Elizabeth's great Minister, was his guardian. To Southampton Shakespeare dedicated *Venus and Adonis*, which was entered in the Stationers' Register on April 18, 1593. Just over a year later, Shakespeare dedicated *Lucrece* to Southampton in warmer terms which suggest that in the interval he had received considerable encouragement. As a young man Southampton was conspicuously handsome, but for some years he refused to marry, although Lord Burleigh himself proposed his own granddaughter as a suitable wife. In 1595, Southampton fell in love with Mistress Elizabeth Vernon, one of Queen Elizabeth's maids of honor, whom, to the Queen's great anger, he secretly married in 1598. Southampton was a personal friend and adoring follower of the Earl of Essex, and shared in his misfortune.[10]

The claims of William Herbert, Earl of Pembroke, are based principally on his initials and on the dedication to him and to his brother of the first folio in 1623, in which Heming and Condell[11] declare "that their Lordships have been pleased to think these trifles somewhat heretofore, and have

9. by English poets   10. The earl of Essex was Queen Elizabeth's favorite courtier who later performed military tasks poorly and fell into disfavor with the queen. He was executed, but Southampton was spared. 11. fellow actors of Shakespeare and joint editors of the first folio of his plays

prosecuted both them and their Author living with so much favor." In 1595 there was a proposal to betroth Pembroke, then aged fifteen, to the daughter of Sir George Carey, son of the patron of the Lord Chamberlain's Company. Apart from this, there is no further known connection between him and Shakespeare.

With Pembroke, however, is linked the name of Mistress Mary Fitton, another of Queen Elizabeth's maids of honor. She was a lively lady who became the mother of three illegitimate children by different men, but afterward married richly and died very respectable. Pembroke was the father of her first child and there was much scandal in court about their behavior. Mistress Fitton is a candidate for the doubtful honor of being considered the "Dark Lady"; she was not, however, conspicuously dark. This theory is known as the "Herbert theory.". . .

There are many other theories, but until some further definite fact is indisputably established, they must remain theories, and the student of poetry can neglect them all.

The sonnet is one of the most difficult forms for sublime or permanent poetry. It is admirable for saying something short, pretty, effective, complimentary, but its very formality and rigidity are against it. There are very few perfect sonnets. The normal form is fixed at fourteen lines of iambic pentameters and a poet cannot always pack or expand his thoughts into so exact a mold. Moreover, Shakespeare chose the most difficult kind of sonnet pattern—three quatrains followed by a couplet. When successful, the couplet folds up the whole poem in a neat final conclusion, but too often the couplet is an awkward appendix to a twelve-line poem.

Shakespeare's sonnets, as poetry, are perhaps rather for private reading than public discussion, for they touch sensitive readers in secret ways. To such readers all discussion of the problems is impertinent and all criticism superfluous.

Evaluating Shakespeare's Sonnets as Poetry

W.H. Auden

Poet W.H. Auden dismisses critics who try to identify
the anonymous man and woman in Shakespeare's
sonnets or determine the order in which the sonnets
belong because neither issue can be proved. Instead,
he turns his attention to the quality of the poetry,
arguing that 49 of the 154 sonnets are wholly
admirable and many more of them are memorable
for particular lines. Auden admires Shakespeare's
mastery of musical and rhetorical devices and cites
examples of both.

W.H. Auden, a twentieth-century American poet
born in England, wrote poems of social criticism in
his early years. His later work abandons his early
themes and focuses on Christian commitment. He
was elected Professor of Poetry at Oxford University
from 1956 to 1960, and for most of his life maintained residences both in the United States and in
Europe. *The Dyer's Hand*, Auden's collected essays,
was published in 1963.

Probably, more nonsense has been talked and written, more
intellectual and emotional energy expended in vain, on the
sonnets of Shakespeare than on any other literary work in
the world. Indeed, they have become the best touchstone I
know of for distinguishing the sheep from the goats, those,
that is, who love poetry for its own sake and understand its
nature, from those who only value poems either as historical documents or because they express feelings or beliefs of
which the reader happens to approve. It so happens that we
know almost nothing about the historical circumstances
under which Shakespeare wrote these sonnets: we don't

Excerpted from the Introduction by W.H. Auden to *Sonnets: The Complete Non-
Dramatic Poetry* by William Shakespeare, edited by William Burto, with an introduc-
tion by W.H. Auden. Copyright ©1964 by William Burto. Copyright ©1963 by Sylvan
Barnet. Introduction copyright ©1964 by W.H. Auden. Used by permission of Dutton
Signet, a division of Penguin Books USA Inc.

know to whom they are addressed or exactly when they were written, and, unless entirely new evidence should turn up, which is unlikely, we never shall. . . .

Let us, however, forget all about Shakespeare the man, leave the speculations about the persons involved, the names, already or in the future to be put forward, Southampton, Pembroke, Hughes, etc., to the foolish and the idle, and consider the sonnets themselves.

The first thing which is obvious after reading through the one hundred and fifty-four sonnets as we have them, is that they are not in any kind of planned sequence. The only semblance of order is a division into two unequal heaps—Sonnets 1 to 126 are addressed to a young man, assuming, which is probable but not certain, that there is only one young man addressed, and Sonnets 127–154 are addressed to a dark-haired woman. . . .

A number of scholars have tried to rearrange the sonnets into some more logical order, but such efforts can never be more than conjecture, and it is best to accept the jumble we have been given.

THE UNEVEN QUALITY OF THE SONNETS

If the first impression made by the sonnets is of their haphazard order, the second is of their extremely uneven poetic value.

After the 1609 edition, the sonnets were pretty well forgotten for over a century and a half. In 1640 Benson produced an extraordinary hodgepodge in which one hundred and forty-six of them were arranged into seventy-two poems with invented titles, and some of the *he*'s and *him*'s changed to *she*'s and *her*'s. It was not until 1780 that a significant critical text was made by Malone[1]. This happened to be a period when critics condemned the sonnet as a form. Thus Steevens[2] could write in 1766:

> Quaintness, obscurity, and tautology[3] are to be regarded as the constituent parts of this exotic species of composition. . . . I am one of those who should have wished it to have expired in the country where it was born. . . . [A sonnet] is composed in the highest strain of affectation, pedantry,[4] circumlocution,[5] and nonsense.

1. literary critic and Shakespearean scholar Edmond   2. Shakespearean critic George
3. use of unnecessary, repetitious words   4. school-bookish rules of verse   5. roundabout ways of explaining meaning

And of Shakespeare's essays in this form:

> The strongest act of Parliament that could be framed would fail to compel readers unto their service.

Even when this prejudice against the sonnet as such had begun to weaken, and even after Bardolatry[6] had begun, adverse criticism of the sonnets continued.

Thus Wordsworth,[7] who was as responsible as anyone for rehabilitating the sonnet as a form (though he employed the Petrarchan, not the Shakespearean, kind), remarked:

> These sonnets beginning at CXXVII to his mistress are worse than a puzzle-peg. They are abominably harsh, obscure, and worthless. The others are for the most part much better, have many fine lines and passages. They are also in many places warm with passion. Their chief faults—and heavy ones they are—are sameness, tediousness, quaintness, and elaborate obscurity.

Hazlitt:[8]

> If Shakespeare had written nothing but his sonnets ... he would ... have been assigned to the class of cold, artificial writers, who had no genuine sense of nature or passion.

Keats:[9]

> They seem to be full of fine things said unintentionally—in the intensity of working out conceits.

Landor:[10]

> Not a single one is very admirable. . . . They are hot and pothery:[11] there is much condensation, little delicacy; like raspberry jam without cream, without crust, without bread; to break its viscidity.[12]

In [the twentieth] century we have reacquired a taste for the conceit, as we have for baroque architecture, and no longer think that artifice is incompatible with passion. Even so, no serious critic of poetry can possibly think that all the sonnets are equally good.

On going through the hundred and fifty-four of them, I find forty-nine which seem to me excellent throughout, a good number of the rest have one or two memorable lines, but there are also several which I can only read out of a sense of duty. For the inferior ones we have no right to condemn Shakespeare unless we are prepared to believe, a belief for which there is no evidence, that he prepared or intended them all to be published.

---

6. time when study of lyric poets, the Bards, became popular   7. English poet William
8. essayist and critic William   9. English poet John   10. English writer Walter Savage
11. overly concerned with trivial matters   12. thick and sticky quality

PETRARCHAN VERSUS SHAKESPEAREAN SONNET FORM

Considered in the abstract, as if they were Platonic Ideas,[13] the Petrarchan sonnet seems to be a more esthetically satisfying form than the Shakespearean. Having only two different rhymes in the octave and two in the sestet, each is bound by rhyme into a closed unity, and the asymmetrical relation of 8 to 6 is pleasing. The Shakespearean form, on the other hand, with its seven different rhymes, almost inevitably becomes a lyric of three symmetrical quatrains, finished off with an epigrammatic couplet. As a rule Shakespeare shapes his rhetorical argument in conformity with this, that is to say, there is usually a major pause after the fourth, the eighth, and the twelfth line. Only in one case, Sonnet 86, "Was it the proud full sail of his great verse," does the main pause occur in the middle of the second quatrain, so that the sonnet divides into 6.6.2.

It is the concluding couplet in particular which, in the Shakespearean form, can be a snare. The poet is tempted to use it, either to make a summary of the preceding twelve lines which is unnecessary, or to draw a moral which is too glib and trite. In the case of Shakespeare himself, though there are some wonderful couplets, for example the conclusion of 61,

> For thee watch I, whilst thou dost wake elsewhere,
> From me far off, with others all too near,

or 87,

> Thus have I had thee as a dream doth flatter,
> In sleep a king, but waking no such matter,

all too often, even in some of the best, the couplet lines are the weakest and dullest in the sonnet, and, coming where they do at the end, the reader has the sense of a disappointing anticlimax.

Despite all this, it seems to me wise of Shakespeare to have chosen the form he did rather than the Petrarchan. Compared with Italian, English is so poor in rhymes that it is almost impossible to write a Petrarchan sonnet in it that sounds effortless throughout. In even the best examples ... one is almost sure to find at least one line the concluding word of which does not seem inevitable, the only word which could accurately express the poet's meaning; one

---

13. expressing universal truths or ideas

SHAKESPEARE'S ART IN SONNET 18

W.H. Auden cites the following sonnet, No. 18, to illustrate Shakespeare's artistic poetic qualities: the opening simile, the beautiful imagery, and examples taken from nature.

Shall I compare thee to a summer's day?
Thou art more lovely and more temperate.
Rough winds do shake the darling buds of May,
And summer's lease hath all too short a date.
Sometime too hot the eye of heaven[1] shines,
And often is his gold complexion dimm'd;
And every fair from fair sometime declines,
By chance, or nature's changing course, untrimm'd;[2]
But thy eternal summer shall not fade
Nor lose possession of that fair thou ow'st,[3]
Nor shall Death brag thou wand'rest in his shade
When in eternal lines to time thou grow'st.
　So long as men can breathe or eyes can see,
　So long lives this, and this gives life to thee.

1. the sun　2. shorn of beauty　3. beauty you possess

feels it is only there because the rhyme demanded it.

In addition, there are certain things which can be done in the Shakespearean form which the Petrarchan, with its sharp division between octave and sestet, cannot do. In Sonnet 66, "Tired with all these, for restful death I cry," and 129, "Th' expense of spirit in a waste of shame," Shakespeare is able to give twelve single-line *exempla* of the wretchedness of this world and the horrors of lust, with an accumulative effect of great power.

In their style, two characteristics of the sonnets stand out. Firstly, their *cantabile*.[14] They are the work of someone whose ear is unerring. In his later blank verse, Shakespeare became a master of highly complicated effects of sound and rhythm, and the counterpointing of these with the sense, but in the sonnets he is intent upon making his verse as melodious, in the simplest and most obvious sense of the word, as possible, and there is scarcely a line, even in the dull ones, which sounds harsh or awkward. Occasionally, there are lines which foreshadow the freedom of his later verse. For example:

14. in a singing manner

> Not mine own fears nor the prophetic soul
> Of the wide world dreaming on things to come.   (107)

But, as a rule, he keeps the rhythm pretty close to the metrical base. Inversion, except in the first foot, is rare, and so is trisyllabic substitution. The commonest musical devices are alliteration—

> Then were not summer's distillation left,
> A liquid prisoner pent in walls of glass   (5)

> Let me not to the marriage of true minds
> Admit impediments . . .   (116)

and the careful patterning of long and short vowels—

> How many a holy and obsequious tear   (31)

> Nor think the bitterness of absence sour   (57)

> So far from home into my deeds to pry.   (61)

The second characteristic they display is a mastery of every possible rhetorical device. The reiteration, for example, of words with either an identical or a different meaning—

> love is not love
> Which alters when it alteration finds,
> Or bends with the remover to remove.   (116)

Or the avoidance of monotony by an artful arithmetical variation of theme or illustration.

Here, I cannot do better than to quote (interpolating lines where appropriate) Professor C.S. Lewis on Sonnet 18. "As often," he says, "the theme begins at line 9,

> But thy eternal summer shall not fade,

occupying four lines, and the application is in the couplet:

> So long as men can breathe or eyes can see,
> So long lives this, and this gives life to thee.

Line 1

> Shall I compare thee to a summer's day

proposes a simile. Line 2

> Thou art more lively and more temperate

corrects it. Then we have two one-line *exempla* justifying the correction,

> Rough winds do shake the darling buds of May,
> And summer's lease hath all too short a date:

then a two-line *exemplum* about the sun,

> Sometime too hot the eye of heaven shines,
> And often is his gold complexion dimmed:

then two more lines,

> And every fair from fair sometime declines,
> By chance, or nature's changing course, untrimmed

which do not, as we had expected, add a fourth *exemplum* but generalize. Equality of length in the two last variations is thus played off against difference of function."

The visual imagery is usually drawn from the most obviously beautiful natural objects, but, in a number, a single metaphorical conceit is methodically worked out, as in 87,

> Farewell, thou art too dear for my possessing,

where the character of an emotional relationship is worked out in terms of a legal contract.

In the inferior sonnets, such artifices may strike the reader as artificial, but he must reflect that, without the artifice, they might be much worse than they are. The worst one can say, I think, is that rhetorical skill enables a poet to write a poem for which genuine inspiration is lacking which, had he lacked such skill, he would not have written at all.

On the other hand those sonnets which express passionate emotions, whether of adoration or anger or grief or disgust, owe a very great deal of their effect precisely to Shakespeare's artifice, for without the restraint and distancing which the rhetorical devices provide, the intensity and immediacy of the emotion might have produced, not a poem, but an embarrassing "human document." Wordsworth defined poetry as emotion recollected in tranquillity. It seems highly unlikely that Shakespeare wrote many of these sonnets out of recollected emotion. In his case, it is the artifice that makes up for the lack of tranquillity. . . .

Perhaps Hannah Arendt is right: "Poets are the only people to whom love is not only a crucial but an indispensable experience, which entitles them to mistake it for a universal one." In Shakespeare's case, what happened to his relations with his friend and his mistress, whether they were abruptly broken off in a quarrel, or slowly faded into indifference, is anybody's guess. Did Shakespeare later feel that the anguish at the end was not too great a price to pay for the glory of the initial vision? I hope so and believe so. Anyway, poets are tough and can profit from the most dreadful experiences.

Shakespeare Used Ordinary Experiences to Create Powerful Sonnets

John Jay Chapman

John Jay Chapman argues that Shakespeare's sonnets are not autobiographical. Chapman presents
Shakespeare as a man of keen vision, one who could
see a powerful idea or emotion in the most trivial in-
cident. Moreover, Chapman argues, Shakespeare was
incomparably talented at turning mundane observations into poetry that displays an unusual facility
with language, as if words were toys in his mind. The
outcome, Chapman maintains, is a series of lyrics on
love which stir readers' most intimate feelings.

John Jay Chapman was an American literary
critic, translator, essayist, playwright, and poet of the
late nineteenth and early twentieth centuries. His
criticism is based on the individualist philosophy of
American writer Ralph Waldo Emerson.

Although no one knows how Shakespeare was employed between the ages of twenty and twenty-eight, when he
emerged as an actor and dramatist, it would seem that the
playhouse was his university. He was dipped in the theatri-
cal business at so early an age that its conventions formed
and controlled his thought. . . .

The stage became his education; the drama was his life.
We are puzzled by this—we who have been taught to see life
as politics, religion, or morality; as conduct, or economics.
We insist that there must have been some part of Shakespeare that we could meet outside his playhouse; and we almost resent the fact that he has no private opinions, and ask
petulantly, "What did the man do for the rest of the day after

Excerpted from "Sonnets," in *A Glance Toward Shakespeare* by John Jay Chapman
(Boston: Atlantic Monthly Press, 1922).

his playwriting was finished?" Well, he staged-managed a theatre, acted in plays, and went to the tavern to meet his friends. That is all that we positively know about him. Between the cavern[1] and the tavern Shakespeare was content. He belonged to that class of artists who live for their work, . . . and as his work was from the start very much appreciated, and he was, moreover, of a most happy disposition, he had no temptation to fume and worry, to wonder whether it was good, to struggle and suffer and write letters, and in one way or another to expose his own relation to his art. If he had any feelings about himself and his work, he worked them off, as he did the rest of his thoughts, in depicting stage characters.

A TRIBUTE TO THE SONNETS

In his book Table Talk, *English Romantic poet Samuel Taylor Coleridge pays tribute to the richness, the thought, and the poetic "sweetness" of Shakespeare's sonnets.*

[Shakespeare's] extraordinary sonnets form in fact a Poem of so many stanzas of fourteen lines each; and like the Passion which inspired them, the sonnets are always the same with a variety of expression—continuous if you regard the Lover's soul, distinct if you listen to him as he heaves them sigh after sigh.

These Sonnets, like the Venus and Adonis and Rape of Lucrece, are characterized by boundless fertility, and labored condensation of thought, with perfection of sweetness in rhythm and metre. These are the essentials in the budding of a great Poet.

That Shakespeare excited so little notice while he lived, and left so few personal records behind him, is indeed puzzling; but then we have no one with whom to compare him. Perhaps men like Shakespeare always live and die unnoticed. . . . Shakespeare's mental grasp, facility, and learning so amaze us that he seems like a creature from another planet; and yet we are forced to judge him by our own. His dramas throw no direct light on his life; nor do the two romantic poems, "Venus and Adonis" and "Lucrece," for these poems are obviously pieces of formal art. Therefore the fam-

1. the theater

ished curiosity of the world has fixed itself upon his Sonnets.

A convention of heavy-footed critics, with shovels on their shoulders and cans of dynamite at their elbows, have been encamped about Shakespeare's Sonnets for a century. They feel that they are about to excavate Shakespeare, and set him up definitively in their museum. They think that, if they but knew the facts of his life, and the identity of W.H., to whom the Sonnets are dedicated, they would pluck out the heart of his mystery and write their names on his tomb. But the mystery of the Sonnets is a mystery that can be delved into only by imaginative perceptions. . . .

The sonnet throughout its history had remained a highly specialized type of literary performance, conventional, candied, and dealing with conceits which had become common property. The vast authority of Petrarch controlled its form and substance for two centuries before Shakespeare's time. . . .

THE FRESH LANGUAGE OF SHAKESPEARE'S SONNETS

There is, however, a difference between the Elizabethan sonnets and their continental forerunners which has not been sufficiently noticed by the scholars. The language of the continental sonneteers was more archaic than that of their British followers. In old Italian and old French sonnets the roses are wired upon an idiom which explains the pose and foundation of the whole art. Had Shakespeare adopted the Italian form of the sonnet, or used an archaic or mannered vehicle, as Dante does in his "Vita Nuova" or Ronsard in his Sequences, the difficulty of interpreting his Sonnets would vanish. We should accept them as things of exotic beauty, impersonal and symbolic, which derive their immortality from the intellect and make appeal to the intellect. But Shakespeare's Sonnets are written in the most ruddy, fluent, spontaneous, inspired vernacular that the English language can show. Their frequent anticlimaxes, their constant carelessness, their monotonies, their absurdities, are sustained and floated on a lyrical genius of the first order. There is no poetry in the world quite like them. Shakespeare thus turned the sonnet into something it had never been before; for its ideas and conceits remain absolutely impersonal and supersensuous, while its language has become warm, rippling, and offhand.

It is wonderful that the single bit of Elizabethan gossip

that has come down to us should give us what we most want
to know about Shakespeare's Sonnets, namely, "how they
struck a contemporary." In 1598 Francis Meres, in reviewing
current poetry, wrote that "the sweet and witty soul of Ovid
lives in mellifluous and honey-tongued Shakespeare, witness his 'Venus and Adonis,' his 'Lucrece' and his sugred
sonnets among his private friends." Sugar'd sonnets among
his private friends! I doubt whether anything has ever been
said about Shakespeare's Sonnets that explains them better
than these six words. Open them anywhere, and lines or
phrases of such rapturous felicity[2] greet us that we seem to
hear the wren.

> Mark how one string, sweet husband to another,
> Strikes each in each by mutual ordering;
> Resembling sire and child and happy mother,
> Who all in one, one pleasing note do sing.
>
> . . . .
> When forty summers shall besiege thy brow,
>
> . . . .
> Shall I compare thee to a summer's day?
>
> . . . .
> When to the sessions of sweet silent thought

The Sonnets should be dipped into, or read by the half-
hour together, singly or in sequences, and without any special effort to understand them; for they have been written in
a mood of quietude and relaxation, perhaps the gentlest
mood that the gentlest poet ever knew. . . .

Shakespeare is expressing a mood which he understands,
has felt, when or how we know not—perhaps only in that
heaven of invention[3] where he found Romeo, Imogen, and
King Lear. The Shakespeare of the Sonnets is merely one of
Shakespeare's characters, and he sprang out of the book and
volume of Shakespeare's brain,—out of all the trivial, fond
records that youth and observation copied there,—even as
Romeo, Imogen, or King Lear sprang from the same source.
And this personage of the Sonnets disappeared—just as
Romeo, Imogen, and King Lear disappeared—with the occasion that gave each of them birth. Just what the circumstances were that gave rise to the Sonnets we do not know;
but even if we knew all their details, we should still have to
understand them by a light which we are apt to forget—the
light of The Sonnet.

2. ecstatic happiness   3. imagination

Shakespeare's Sonnets were almost certainly paid for by his patron, and were certainly handed about freely among the wits of the time. To our taste it seems absurd that Shakespeare should have written seventeen sonnets to a young nobleman, beseeching the lad to beget children in order that his beauty might be transmitted to posterity. But we must remember that the exchange of absurd sonnets was a social game, lately introduced from France, which everyone was playing when Shakespeare wrote. I can go as far as believing that the pampered boy was handsome, . . . but I cannot believe that Shakespeare was sincerely anxious about the continuance of the human species by this youth. If it were the case of Tennyson, I should believe every word the poet said. I should be surprised, of course, that any man should have strong feelings about such a matter; but I should accept Tennyson's word for it. In the case of Shakespeare, however, I feel that what the sociologists call the "play-instinct" is involved. To speak brutally, it is a joke. . . .

THE SONNETS ORIGINATE IN SHAKESPEARE'S IMAGINATION

Now it is natural to suppose that Shakespeare, having discovered a new talent in himself in writing the first seventeen Sonnets, proceeded to write many more in the same manner. The order in which they are printed is not quite authoritative, for they are supposed to have been published piratically by the booksellers. The general theme of them is the celebration of ideal love—precisely the theme of Dante and of Petrarch. The mood they depict is not the mood of one who is in love, but the mood of one who knows what love is. . . .

The biographical value of the Sonnets is that they show how slight was the occasion out of which Shakespeare, through his passion for abstractions, was able to draw those pictures of love-in-absence, lovers' quarrels, love at unequal ages, love's forgivenesses, love's happiness, which have been the comfort of lovers of both sexes ever since. . . .

Each of these gentle sonnets is a toy of the brain made to express the abstraction. But it is a toy like the mariner's needle, with which the whole of earth and all the heavens are in conspiracy. A current of gigantic power is running through these toys. Shakespeare himself, though he knows they are toys, does not know they are powerful. He thinks he is merely giving to airy nothings a local habitation and a name. . . .

He eludes us in the Sonnets as completely as in the plays,

and for the same reason: his mind had the power of grasp-ing abstractions that are larger than we can compass. We are led to suspect that a brain such as his *could* not evolve the personal; he translated it into an abstraction as soon as he saw it. In the process of expressing a private opinion, he turned it into a generality, and this habit became so inveter-ate[4] with him, and he became so alarmingly clever, so com-pletely absorbed in the explosions of his thought at each mo-ment, that we are shaken and surprised, as perhaps he was; but it is only the universal in ourselves which is touched. It is the impersonal, the divine, that we get from him, whether in play or sonnet. We find our own intimate thoughts in him.

4. confirmed

CHAPTER 2

Poetic Techniques Used in the Sonnets

READINGS ON
THE SONNETS

Some Sonnets Express Mixed Feelings

Hilton Landry

Hilton Landry argues that some of Shakespeare's sonnets express mixed feelings. Landry illustrates this observation by analyzing Sonnets 57 and 58, both of which portray the poet in a master-slave relationship with the young man he addresses. In Sonnet 57, because the poet is a slave to love, he endures the misery of waiting for the friend to return and give another command. As a true servant, however, he sees no injustice in having to wait. In Sonnet 58, the speaker waits and suffers in silence while the friend takes his pleasures, but, again, as a slave to love, he expresses no complaint or disapproval of the friend's unrestrained behavior, his "libertinism."

Hilton Landry has taught English at Kent State University in Kent, Ohio, and the University of California at Davis. He has published two books on Shakespeare's sonnets, edited a volume on old and rare books, and published a concordance to the poems of American poet Hart Crane.

The speaker's mixed feelings about his friend, his simultaneous liking and disliking, his being attracted and repelled, are apparent in [several sonnets]. The negative component of this ambivalence is perceptibly stronger than the positive one, and indeed it seems reasonable to suppose that in most instances of ambivalence one state of mind will outweigh the other. . . . Although both affection and antagonism may be quite evident, the poet at different times seems to give more emphasis to either his positive or negative feelings. . . .

Sonnets 57 and 58 concern a master-slave relationship in which the speaker plays the unhappy role of the slave of love, disliking his servile dependence and the bitterness of

Excerpted from *Interpretations in Shakespeare's Sonnets: A Critical Introduction* by Hilton Landry (Berkeley & Los Angeles: University of California Press, 1963). Copyright ©1963 by The Regents of the University of California. Reprinted with permission of the publisher.

his friend's absence without being able to escape from emotional domination. His resentment is realized by the sense, tone, and feeling of the Sonnets, by an obvious and bitter irony. Both Sonnets convey the misery of the true and watchful servant. . . .

THE MISERY OF BEING A SLAVE TO LOVE

In Sonnet 57 the implications of an initial generalization (in the form of a rhetorical question) are made clear by the particulars of succeeding lines, and the irony which is directed chiefly at his friend is also aimed at the poet himself.

> Being your slave, what should I do but tend
> Upon the hours and times of your desire?
> I have no precious time at all to spend,
> 4   Nor services to do, till you require.
> Nor dare I chide the world-without-end hour
> Whilst I, my sovereign, watch the clock for you,
> Nor think the bitterness of absence sour
> 8   When you have bid your servant once adieu.
> Nor dare I question with my jealous thought
> Where you may be, or your affairs suppose,
> But, like a sad slave, stay and think of nought
> 12   Save where you are how happy you make those.
>   So true a fool is love that in your will,
>   Though you do anything, he thinks no ill.

He begins by asking a question needing no answer: As your abject inferior, subservient to your will, what ought I to do except be (always) ready to serve you whenever you want something (whenever you are through satisfying your appetites, your other needs and longings that have nothing to do with me)? In fact, he continues, I have no time to spend that seems valuable (to me), and no services to perform for you until you ask or demand them. (I would like to have the opportunity to do the things for you that *my* loving friendship prompts me to, but you avoid me until you have some demand to make and thus cause me to waste a great deal of my time.)

"The hours and times of your desire," built on a formula that is a hallmark of Shakespeare's style, is deliberately ambiguous, enabling the poet to refer to different aspects of the same situation. It obviously points to the friend's demands on the speaker, with "desire" (wish, request, demand) looking forward to "require," and "hours and times" implying the few hours and occasions on which friendship is served. And despite the silence of the commentators, it also calls attention to the friend's neglect of the poet. In this sense the phrase is equivalent to "your times of pleasure" in Sonnet 58; "desire" (sensual appetite, lust) anticipates "will," and "hours and times" refers to the "world-without-end" hours and many occasions devoted to the pursuit of pleasure.

The irony of the second quatrain, which bears out my reading of "hours and times" and lines 3–4, is straightforward: I dare not curse the tedium of waiting for you, my lord and master, or even think that your absence is bitter. The striking compound in the phrase "the world-without-end hour" (l. 5), used by Shakespeare in only one other place, may remind one of the phrase "world without end" which occurs in the *Gloria Patri* and the hymn *Te Deum Laudamus*[1] of the Book of Common Prayer, as well as in Isaiah 45:17:

> Glory be to the Father, and to the Sonne: and to the
> holy Ghost
> As it was in the beginning, is nowe, and ever shal be:
> world without end.
> We magnifie thee day by day,
> and world withouten end:
> Adore thy holy name, O Lord
> vouchsafe us to defend
> From sinne this day, have mercy Lord,
> have mercy on us all:
> And on us as we trust in thee,
> Lord let thy mercy fall.

> But Israel shall be saved in the Lord, with an everlasting
> salvation: yee shall not be ashamed nor confounded, world
> without ende.

Perhaps one or more of these familiar passages suggested the phrase as a vivid means of conveying everlastingness, the psychological truth that when we are waiting for someone to come or for something to happen, with all our attention and energy directed toward that moment, even an hour seems endless. Here as in *Love's Labor's Lost* (V.ii.797)[2] Shakespeare thinks of love as "a world-without-end bargain," and, because it is, the enslaved speaker cannot hope that he "shall not be ashamed nor confounded world without ende."

With the last quatrain the speaker's irony returns more forcibly upon himself. He says, I dare not consider too care-

---

1. songs in the liturgy praising God
2. KING. Now, at the latest minute of the hour,
   Grant us your loves.
   PRINCESS.   A time, methinks, too short
       To make a word-without-end bargain in.

fully with my justifiably suspicious mind where you may be, or form too clear an idea of your affairs, for your sake as well as my own; instead, like a sorrowful and serious slave I wait for your return and think of nothing except how happy you make those who are with you—wherever you are. He cannot help thinking of what his friend is doing—indeed, in a general way he knows—but to preserve his self-respect he dare not inquire too closely.

A Play on "Will"

Ambiguous in syntax and diction, the couplet summarizes his view of his slavery. There are at least three ways of taking it: (a) So true a fool is love that in your Will (the poet) / Though you do anything, he thinks no ill; (b) So true a fool is love that, though you do anything, he thinks no ill in your will; (c) So true a fool is love that, though you do anything in your will, he thinks no ill. Since all these readings are consonant with the poem as a whole, there is no need of favoring any one of them to the exclusion of the others. The Quarto's[3] "Will" invites us to regard it as the poet's name or a play on his name in the manner of Sonnets 135 and 136, "Whoever hath her wish, thou hast thy Will," and "If thy soul check thee that I come so near"; so faithful and genuine a fool is love that in the person of your friend Will he thinks there is no harm in whatever you do. In the second meaning of the line the constant fool who is the loving speaker thinks the friend's *intentions* are good, or rather not bad, whatever he does. This may also be a way of uttering a hoary commonplace by way of an excuse—that the volitional faculty itself is always directed at what seems to be the good.[4]

> The will, because of an instinct implanted in it by God, desires the good and abhors the evil which the reason represents to it. The will is sometimes called the rational appetite because it desires the good just as the sensitive affections desire the pleasing, and it abhors the evil just as they abhor the displeasing.

According to the third reading, so loyal a fool is love that whatever the friend does that lies within his power of choosing, or in his willfulness or perversity, in his lust, the speaker thinks there is no evil in it.

---

3. the publication of 1609   4. The notion that humans desire good and avoid evil goes back to Greek philosophers Socrates and Plato. Here, Lawrence Babb explains the idea in *The Elizabethan Malady*.

Setting aside the significance of "fool" for the moment, it is clear that "true" denotes loyal, constant, faithful, as well as real or genuine. Neither sense can be dispensed with, for although the speaker intends the phrase to convey strong self-reproach (So big a fool am I), the fool's loyalty to his friend is the basis of their relationship. Playing on the poet's name, "will" has all these senses: the volitional part of the rational soul, the power of choosing and willing; choice, wish, pleasure, desire; intention; willfulness or perversity; lust. Both "anything" and "he" are emphatic, and "ill" signifies (moral) evil, sin; harm, injury. There is an implicit disparity between what he, as opposed to others, thinks of his friend's intentions and actions. As a true fool he may see no personal injury, no sin against friendship, in them, but others who can see things objectively probably regard them as both morally evil and injurious to the speaker.

THE POET AS FOOL

Here and elsewhere in the Sonnets the fool is one who has been made a fool of (by Love or Time), who is somebody's or something's dupe or sport: "Love's not Time's fool" (116); "the fools of Time" (124); "Thou blind fool, Love, what dost thou to mine eyes / That they behold and see not what they see?" (137). On the most obvious level, then, the speaker qualifies as a fool because he is stupid enough to be duped by love, which is traditionally blind. He is also a servant or slave, a talker, and a condoner of sin, roles which further entitle him to be called "fool." In relation to his sovereign he is something like a court fool—a privileged familiar who can say almost anything but is nevertheless a mere servant. Much as he dislikes his situation, as a slave he can only think and talk about it, complain at length but take no action. In this respect he is a talker (rather than a doer), and to talk is characteristic of the fool, as both etymology and the Bible suggest. "Fool" derives from a Latin word for bellows which in late Latin became windbag, fool; and a number of passages in Proverbs and Ecclesiastes remind us that "a fool . . . is full of words." In the Bible "fool" often signifies sinner, a sense that fits the poet to the extent that he sins in condoning ill, corrupting himself by salving the friend's amiss.[5]

To connive and wink at your friend's weaknesses, to gloss

---

5. an idea expressed by Dutch humanist Erasmus in *The Praise of Folly*

them over and to be taken in by them, even to admire and love his worst faults as if they were virtues—doesn't this look like folly?

Yet in the final analysis perhaps it is the friend who is the fool and the speaker who is wise, for in the Socratic view to know you are a fool is a sign of wisdom.

WAITING AND SUFFERING IN SILENCE

Pooler[6] describes the equivocal Sonnet 58 as a "complaint in the form of an assertion that he has no right to complain"; Empson[7] agrees that it is "two-faced in idea."

> That god forbid that made me first your slave
> I should in thought control your times of pleasure,
> Or at your hand th' account of hours to crave,
> 4   Being your vassal bound to stay your leisure!
> 0, let me suffer (being at your beck)
> Th' imprisoned absence of your liberty;[8]
> And patience, tame to sufferance, bide each check[9]
> 8   Without accusing you of injury.
> Be where you list; your charter is so strong
> That you yourself may privilege your time
> To what you will; to you it doth belong
> 12   Yourself to pardon of self-doing crime.
>   I am to wait, though waiting so be hell;
>   Not blame your pleasure, be it ill or well.

It opens with a statement put in an ironic, almost sarcastic, optative mood: may the god (of love) that first made me your slave forbid that I should, *even in thought*, control the occasions of your pleasure, the times devoted to enjoyment, amusement, gratification (whether sensuous or sensual), to doing whatever you want to do; or that I should beg for an accounting of how you spend your time, for I am only your servant, obliged to wait till you are unoccupied.

The ironic optative continues in the second quatrain, which apparently stresses the poet's patient servility while it reveals a painful awareness of his grievances. He says, Since I am at your command, let me bear with patience and constancy the pain of the imprisoning absence resulting from your freedom and libertinism; and may my patience, submissive to suffering and pain, endure each rebuke or taunt without accusing you of wrong or insult. Four words in these lines ("suffer," "patience," "sufferance," and "bide") com-

6. C. Knox, editor of *The Works of William Shakespeare: Sonnets,* by Edward Dowden
7. critic William   8. You are free to go as you please, and your absence makes me a prisoner   9. rebuke

bine the notions of experiencing something which causes pain and grief and putting up with, making the best of it. The ostensible emphasis is on toleration, a necessary condition of slavery, but the speaker's sense of injury is equally prominent. Of course the friend has the liberty to be absent, the freedom to do what he wishes, even if absence imprisons the poet by keeping him from his friend. Yet if the friend flaunts his liberty by devoting his absences to libertinism, then it is natural for the speaker to feel wronged ("check," "injury," "crime"). "Check" signifies taunt as well as rebuke or reproof, and, in view of the implications of "pleasure" and "liberty," it probably glances at the term from falconry meaning to stoop for baser game and the baser game itself.

In the third quatrain the friend's rights, already recognized in the references to liberty and pleasure, temporarily come to the fore. The poet says, be where you please; do what you want with your time; forgive yourself for any sin you commit and any injury you do to yourself. As "list" and "will" look backward (and forward) to "pleasure," so "charter" and "privilege" look back to "liberty," for the senses of "liberty" include franchise, privilege, right, as well as freedom and libertinism. "Charter," signifying right or privilege, may also suggest a contract between them, a contract favoring the friend because the speaker's love is so great. Indeed, it is the depth of the poet's love even more than the friend's character that makes one a fool and a slave and gives the other the prerogatives of a king.

The summarizing couplet states the requisites of the poet's position as he derives them from his experience: he is to wait and suffer and to suffer in silence. He must wait, even if it is a veritable hell of anxiety and misery to do so; he must not find fault with the friend's choice, with the gratification, whether good or bad, that keeps the friend from him even though it may be a rebuke or an insult. "Wait" has three senses which sum up the speaker's role with marvelous economy—to wait for, to keep watch, to be on duty or ready to serve; for he is at once the anxious loving friend, the ineffectual observer-guardian of his friend's behavior ("For thee watch I whilst thou dost wake elsewhere, / From me far off, with others all too near"),[10] and his friend's willing (and unwilling) servant.

10. the couplet from Sonnet 61

Shakespeare's Poetic Imagery

W.G. Ingram

W.G. Ingram argues that thought moves forward in
Shakespeare's sonnets by means of imagery. Shakespeare does not express ideas and emotions in clear,
logically developed sentences. Rather, he engages the
reader's imagination to see and feel meaning by con-
necting one image with another. Ingram analyzes several sonnets to illustrate different patterns in which
the images connect and advance ideas. For example, a
sonnet might begin with a general idea and move to a
particular experience, or vice versa, or evolve, each
new image suggested by the previous one.

W.G. Ingram was a lecturer on English literature
at Trinity College and a director of English studies at
Emmanuel College, both in Cambridge, England, before teaching at the University of Michigan at Ann
Arbor. He has written essays on the theater as well
as literary criticism.

In studies of the Sonnets we naturally find attention directed
to their imagery; but the interest has been largely thematic.
Its effect on structure and on what I will call "movement" *in-
side* the sonnet form—on the nature of the thought progression that modifies content-pattern—has received but limited
notice. Yet this is one of the features that markedly distin-
guish the "Shakespearean" feel of the Sonnets from the general run of contemporary sonneteering. . . .

One element of the characteristic Shakespearean quality
can be found in what I have already called the movement of
the sonnet, the thought progression that is an essential element of its structure as a poem, as distinct from the merely
formal patterning of lines and rhyme scheme; and this
thought progression is essentially linked with the way Shake-

Excerpted from "The Shakespeare Quality" by W.G. Ingram, in *New Essays on Shakespeare's Sonnets*, edited by Hilton Landry (New York: AMS Press, 1976). Copyright
©1976 by AMS Press, Inc. Reprinted with permission from the publisher.

speare's mind works in the deployment and development of the imagery. . . .

SONNET 12: FROM FAMILIAR OBJECT TO PROFOUND IDEA

It is the difference of impact, and with it the whole progression of the sonnet, that ring deeper tones in Shakespeare's work. . . .

> When I do count the clock that tells the time.
> And see the brave day sunk in hideous night;
> When I behold the violet past prime
> 4   And sable curls o'er-silver'd all with white;
> When lofty trees I see barren of leaves,
> Which erst from heat did canopy the herd,
> And summer's green all girded up in sheaves
> 8   Borne on the bier with white and bristly beard:[1]
> Then of thy beauty do I question make
> That thou among the wastes of time must go,
> Since sweets and beauties do themselves forsake,
> 12   And die as fast as they see others grow;
>   And nothing 'gainst Time's scythe can make defence
>   Save breed[2] to brave[3] him when he takes thee hence.
>
>   (Sonnet 12)

. . . The progression of [Sonnet 12] has a complexity of verbal and conceptual associations that moves, unobtrusively and compulsively, from the concrete symbols of transience[4] (the clock, the violet) to death, Time, and defiance of mere mortality. Temporality in the first line is simple, measurable, horological:[5] the second line not only compasses the whole passing day but with its powerfully emotive contrast of adjectives ("brave day" and "hideous night") imposes an atmosphere of doom on the commonplace clock that just "tells the time." The next lines carry us further, from the transitory day to the passing seasons of nature and of man, "barren" in line 5 having a thematic undertone relevant to the matter of the first group of sonnets. And with line 8 Shakespeare's habitual verbal associativeness begins to take charge: "bier" seems to suggest to him "beard," and the ripened beards of barley are "white and bristly" with the hoar of age. We have moved from the immediate moment to the recurrent transience of all things, and this leads us into the contemplation of beauty passing "among the wastes of time," and, with the seasonal harvesting or ripened grain, to "Time's scythe.". . .

---

1. the barley, once green, now white and bearded, cut, stacked, and carted   2. offspring   3. taunt   4. time's passing, its temporality   5. as measured by a clock

SONNET 15: FROM GRAND VISION TO INTIMATE FRIENDSHIP

An equally interesting progression is to be found in Sonnet 15. Again the multiple images grow one out of another, and with them this time the thought closes in from the general to the particular, from the world and its transience to the love of friend for friend. The first quatrain, enunciating in its opening lines the universality of transience and decline, in its third and fourth employs a metaphor that presents the general condition of man on an analogical level:

> When I consider everything that grows
> Holds in perfection but a little moment,
> That this huge stage presenteth nought but shows
> Whereon the stars in secret influence[6] comment;

The image of the next quatrain parallels this, but with a difference:

> When I perceive that men as plants increase,
> Cheered and check'd even by the selfsame sky,
> Vaunt in their youthful sap, at height decrease,
> And wear their brave state out of memory:

Where the former image was offered on an analogical level, this one brings man into direct fellowship with the natural world that had stood remote. The sky that commented, though with "secret influence" from a distance, on the "shows" presented on man's worldly state, now cheers and checks the players as directly, as overtly, as the seasons promote and curb the growth of the plant world. (Typically, the image of line 8 derives at least in part from association with the actors in lines 3 and 4; for Elizabethan players frequently wore the finery discarded by noble patrons when fashion had demoded it.) We have moved *on*, not circled by the superficial extension of a conceit; have progressed, not by a logical exploitation of the former image in the manner of, say, Donne,[7] but into a different yet not inconsequent image; and with this progression we have moved deeper and closer into the human condition and the poet's contemplation of it—which is about to become his personal involvement *with* it.

For now follows the sestet:

> Then the conceit of this inconstant stay
> Sets you most rich in youth before my sight,
> Where wasteful time debateth with decay
> To change your day of youth to sullied night;
>   And all in war with Time for love of you,

---

6. In Shakespeare's day, planets were believed to give out a kind of fluid or "influence," which greatly affected humans.   7. poet John

As he takes from you I engraft[8] you new.

The general reflection on man's estate is now applied intimately to the poet, his friend, and the perpetual war of Time with youth and beauty. The vocabulary is still drawn from the world of nature and the universe—day and night and the engrafting of trees. But from the remote impersonal spectatorship of the stars we have moved, through the direct consideration of the human condition, to the active partisanship, in the war against Time, of the love of friend for friend; and it is through the shifting imagery that this movement is effected. This is the functional activity of imagery in pushing the thought-movement forward, not concentrically but in a more complex progression that characterizes a number of Shakespeare's sonnets. . . .

SONNET 60: DISSIMILAR IMAGES
DEVELOP ONE FROM ANOTHER

Probably the most cited, among the Sonnets, as instancing Shakespeare's shifting imagery, as exemplifying what is apparently an almost completely inconsequential sequence of disparates, is Sonnet 60. It is also a striking example of the way the association of image with word and of word with image dictates the patterning of the thought progression while still retaining in fact an inherent unity.

> Like as the waves make towards the pebbled shore,
> So do our minutes hasten to their end;
> Each changing place with that which goes before
> 4   In sequent toil all forwards do contend.
> Nativity,[9] once in the main of light,[10]
> Crawls to maturity, wherewith being crown'd,
> Crookèd eclipses 'gainst his glory fight,
> 8   And Time that gave doth now his gift confound.
> Time doth transfix the flourish set on youth,
> And delves the parallels in beauty's brow,
> Feeds on the rarities of nature's truth;
> 12   And nothing stands but for his scythe to mow.
>   And yet to times in hope my verse shall stand,
>   Praising thy worth, despite his cruel hand.

Beginning with a "straight" simile of the advancing tide creeping imperceptibly on the shore (the advancing tide, for time in Shakespeare is always the destroyer, the eroder), the poem with its succeeding quatrains presents a series of im-

---

8. i.e., graft you into my verse and restore what time has destroyed   9. the moment of birth; i.e., a newborn infant   10. bright daylight

ages that on the literal plane appear inconsistent, but which gain a thematic coherence as one studies how they are produced one from another. From the advancing tide of the sea (a concrete image) we leap first to the abstract nativity (whose submerged concrete association with the newborn babe is implicit, but not explicated, in the verb "crawls"), then to light that is "crowned" with maturity (another concrete / abstract conjunction), to eclipses that "fight" against light's glory, to gifts destroyed by the giver. Time personified is the giver and destroyer of these gifts, but immediately becomes a dart thrower, a digger of trenches, a destroying cankerworm, a reaper. And these are not presented as simple parallels, as a bundle of images.... They grow one out of another in an ever-changing concatenation[11] that may defy logic but leads the mind on emotionally to the climax of line 12....

SONNET 7: A SINGLE IMAGE MOVES DIRECTLY FORWARD

Sonnet 7 provides an example early in the Quarto of a single image developed through the quatrains, with application to its object in the couplet.

> Lo, in the orient when the gracious light
> Lifts up his burning head, each under eye
> Doth homage to his new-appearing sight,
> 4   Serving with looks his sacred majesty;
> And having climb'd the steep-up heavenly hill,
> Resembling strong youth in his middle age,
> Yet mortal looks adore his beauty still,
> 8   Attending on his golden pilgrimage:
> But when from highmost pitch,[12] with weary car,[13]
> Like feeble age he reeleth from the day,
> The eyes ('fore duteous) now converted are
> 12   From his low tract,[14] and look another way:
>   So thou thyself out-going in thy noon,
>   Unlook'd on diest unless thou get[15] a son.

Here the sun-king's daily journey in his chariot is related in three stages, morning, noon, and evening, to mortal homage and to time, age, advance, and decline. The couplet, scarcely epigrammatic, applies this sequence to the state of the willfully heirless friend. The various elements of diction maintain a consonant sequence. "Gracious light," "burning head," "beauty," and "golden" form one, the dawn-to-noon group. "New-appearing," "strong youth," "middle age," and "feeble

11. a series or chain of images   12. zenith; literally, the highest point in the flight of a hawk   13. chariot   14. track   15. beget

age" mark the progression of time, as "Lifts up," "climb'd," "steep-up ... hill," "pilgrimage," "highmost pitch," "weary car," "reeleth," and "low tract" measure it, as it were, spatially along the sun's course. Parallel to this sequence runs the homage group: "homage," "sacred majesty," "adore," "Attending," "eyes ('fore duteous) now converted" to "look another way." (Such a grouping is necessarily too crude, for "gracious" and "golden" belong as much to the last sequence as to the first, just as "reeleth" reverses the motion of "Lifts up" and "climb'd"; and the whole interrelation is equally intricate.) Finally, the couplet picks up the sequence and echoes it: "If you outlast your prime and pass middle age in heirlessness you will die unhonored and unregarded." How clumsily a prose paraphrase destroys the structural link when we lose the verbal echoes of earlier lines with "thou thyself *out-going in thy noon, / Unlook'd on diest.*"

Such a sonnet moves directly forward, through twelve verbally integrated lines, from its developed position to the "application" reached in the couplet. We may regard it as one of the simplest structures, but I have lingered over the word groups to emphasize how, even in so direct a structure, the verbal organization is deliberately controlled. For it is by the variant use of this verbal patterning, combined with the thought progression derived from or controlling his use of imagery, that Shakespeare's art overrides the limitations of the abstract diagram of his prosodic form.

By no means all the sonnets divide simply into octave and sestet, quatrains and couplet, or position, counterposition, and conclusion. Some indeed do proceed, and proceed very effectively, by three stages and a conclusion. Sonnet 7, we have seen, does so in a direct forward movement that is verbally interlocked....

The deployment and thought progressions of the imagery are qualities that Shakespeare develops and utilizes with cogent dramatic efficacy in the verse structure of his plays. This has been extensively studied and expounded elsewhere. They bear relation also to consideration of the Sonnets.

The Speaker in Shakespeare's Sonnets Is Identifiable

Hallett Smith

Hallett Smith agrees neither with those who argue that Shakespeare's sonnets are autobiographical nor with those who insist they are not. Smith proposes that the "I," the speaker in the sonnets, reveals a persona, a character with identifiable traits who represents the poet. He illustrates his point by analyzing sonnets that identify the speaker as victim, actor, one who feels guilty, and a constant lover. Smith argues that by writing sonnets in which an identifiable person addresses a friend, Shakespeare achieves an intimacy that approaches the intimacy of dialogue.

Hallett Smith taught English at Williams College, Williamstown, Massachusetts, and the California Institute of Technology, Pasadena, before becoming research associate at the Huntington Library in San Marino, California. He has edited an anthology of English literature, a collection of critical essays on *The Tempest*, and a collection of Shakespeare's works.

In the sonnets numbered 18–126 in 1609, the Fair Friend is now the beloved of the speaker; he has a personality and a character. The sonnets express over and over again a moral concern about him. Prodigality is not encouraged, it is deplored. Great attention is paid to "inward worth" without neglecting "outward fair" (16.11). Even the conventional praise which promises to confer immortality is different. No longer is there a half-serious rivalry between a son and poetry to perpetuate the beauty of the young man. Poetry has won the contest; it is now the "mightier way" to make war upon that bloody tyrant, Time (16.1–2)....

We must now consider the character of the poet (or

Excerpted from *The Tension of the Lyre: Poetry in Shakespeare's Sonnets* by Hallett Smith (San Marino, CA: Huntington Library Press, 1981). Copyright 1981 by The Huntington Library. Reprinted by permission of the publisher.

speaker) as it is revealed or hinted at in the sonnets. These are lyric poems, love poems associated in a loose way with two traditions, the Petrarchan love sonnet and the epigram tradition. They are not narrative poems. Their principal purpose, their reason for existence, is not to tell a story.

Since most of Shakespeare's work is dramatic, and the dramatist is hidden behind his characters, searchers for a clue to Shakespeare's personality have naturally turned to the sonnets. There they can find almost anything. Some, so literal-minded that their qualifications to read poetry seem very dubious, conclude from Sonnet 37.3, "So I, made lame by Fortune's dearest spite" that the poet suffered an injury to his leg. . . . In actuality, the poet of the sonnets, the "I" who speaks the poems, is rather mysterious. . . . One critic explains: "The reason why the sonnets are the greatest love poems in the language is also the reason why Shakespeare is the greatest poetic dramatist. We could call it selflessness—and the critics have often drawn attention to the lack of self-assertion in Shakespeare's sonnets, compared to those of his contemporaries. We could borrow Keats's phrase and call it 'negative capability.'"

THE PERSONA AS VICTIM

I believe these critics are right in so far as their remarks apply to William Shakespeare, the author of the sonnets and the plays. But the "I" of the sonnets, though mysterious, is not quite so anonymous. He may or may not bear a close resemblance to William Shakespeare, but he is a *persona* with identifiable traits. The first is that he is a victim of circumstances and feels it strongly. Sonnet 29 displays the victim:

> When in disgrace with Fortune and men's eyes
> I all alone beweep my outcast state,
> And trouble deaf heaven with my bootless[1] cries,
> And look upon myself and curse my fate,
> Wishing me like to one more rich in hope,
> Featur'd like him, like him with friends possess'd,
> Desiring this man's art and that man's scope,
> With what I most enjoy contented least;
> Yet in these thoughts myself almost despising,
> Haply I think on thee, and then my state
> (Like to the lark at break of day arising
> From sullen earth) sings hymns at heaven's gate,
>   For thy sweet love rememb'red such wealth brings,
>   That then I scorn to change my state with kings.

1. vain

THE ACTOR PERSONA IN *MACBETH*

In several sonnets, the speaker compares himself to an actor.
Shakespeare also used the persona of an actor in Macbeth.
Near the end of the play, in the following excerpt, Macbeth
says life is a player on a stage.

> Tomorrow, and tomorrow, and tomorrow
> Creeps in this petty pace from day to day,
> To the last syllable of recorded time,
> And all our yesterdays have lighted fools
> The way to dusty death. Out, out, brief candle!
> Life's but a walking shadow, a poor player
> That struts and frets his hour upon the stage
> And then is heard no more. It is a tale
> Told by an idiot, full of sound and fury,
> Signifying nothing.

The first quatrain expresses not only anguish at the
speaker's misfortunes but irritation and boredom at the mul-
tiplicity of them. The lines move urgently, almost without
caesura; the repeated *and* in lines 3 and 4 has the insistence
of a drum beat. *Trouble* is much stronger as a verb than as a
noun, and the assonance of *deaf heaven* as well as its seman-
tic compression has a powerful effect. The *one* in line 5 and
the two *hims* of line 6 are three different people, as the addition of "*this* man's art" and "*that* man's scope" would seem to
confirm. The pointing to five more fortunate men strength-
ens the force of *all alone* and *outcast* in line 2. The thought
turns at the beginning of the sestet with *Yet,* and the image of
the lark at heaven's gate (celebrated again, of course, in the
great aubade[2] in *Cymbeline* II, iii, 20–26) really portrays the
speaker's spirit or mood, called *state* here but preparing for
the double-meaning *state* ("condition" and "throne") in line
14. A very perceptive critic, Stanley Burnshaw, comments on
this third quatrain, "The final figure, a small poem in itself,
sweeps up with suddenness all that preceded. The speaker's
'state' is no longer compared with that of other people, as has
been done up to this point; it *becomes* the lark singing hymns
at the gate of heaven. 'Like' loses its force in the actualization
of the image of soaring. The elements blend together in the
new con-fusion that names a feeling which cannot be named

2. a song about dawn

by other means." A distinguished musicologist once remarked that in the two uses of *state* Shakespeare was modu-
lating from a minor to a major key.

THE PERSONA AS ONE LOWER IN RANK

The contrast between the speaker and more successful or
more prominent people is the basis of other sonnets. Sonnet
25 begins

> Let those who are in favor with their stars[3]
> Of public honor and proud titles boast,
> Whilst I whom fortune of such triumph bars
> Unlook'd for joy in that I honor most.[4]

Honor, the noun in line 2, has quite different associations
from those of *honor* the verb in line 4. This sonnet, too, begins with a tone of complaint about obscurity and failure but
almost immediately concludes with happiness. The poet
does not really envy the court favorite who may lose his
place in the sun at any moment, or the warrior who may
lose all his honors and reputation after one defeat. His love
is returned, and that is enough for him.

Sonnet 91 again makes the contrast:

> Some glory in their birth, some in their skill,
> Some in their wealth, some in their body's force,
> Some in their garments, though new-fangled ill,[5]
> Some in their hawks and hounds, some in their horse;
> And every humor[6] hath his adjunct[7] pleasure,
> Wherein it finds a joy above the rest,
> But these particulars are not my measure,
> All these I better in one general best.
> Thy love is [better] than high birth to me,
> Richer than wealth, prouder than garments' cost,
> Of more delight than hawks or horses be,
> And having thee, of all men's pride I boast:
> >   Wretched in this alone, that thou mayst take
> >   All this away, and me most wretched make.

The reiteration of *Some* in the first quatrain gives an impression of a courtly world where everyone's own disposition leads him to pursue something worldly which gives
him "a joy above the rest." But these are not for the speaker;
they are not his "measure." (One can almost hear the silent
rhyming "treasure.") The rhetorical trick in line 8 of playing
better as a verb against *best* as a noun is followed by the tri-

3. lucky   4. rejoice without notice   5. the latest ugly fashion   6. whim   7. annexed
or connected

umph of *better* as a comparative adjective over *richer*, *prouder*, and *of more delight*, culminating in the "of all men's pride I boast," recalling the "Some glory" of the first line. Finally, by another verbal trick, *wretched* is used in two senses. In line 13 it means "deprived, unfulfilled"; in line 14 it means "miserable."

THE PERSONA AS ACTOR

In one of several sonnets apologizing for not expressing his love more fully, the speaker compares himself to an actor suffering from stage fright:

> As an unperfect actor on the stage
> Who with his fear is put besides his part ...

> (23.1-2)

Since Shakespeare himself was an actor, for part of his career anyway, and lived among actors for all of his years in London, it has been tempting to identify the speaker with William Shakespeare the man. That he should use theater metaphors is natural enough. . . .

It is traditional to see references to Shakespeare's career as an actor in the little series 110–12, though surely something else is involved, too. Just what it is that the speaker is ashamed of is not made clear. Sonnet 110 begins as a rueful confession and ends with a promise of reform. This surely fits something bigger than an actor's life, however disreputable that might have seemed in some Elizabethan circles.

> Alas, 'tis true, I have gone here and there,
> And made myself a motley[8] to the view,
> Gor'd mine own thoughts, sold cheap what is most dear,
> Made old offenses of affections new;[9]
> Most true it is that I have look'd on truth
> Askaunce and strangely: but by all above
> These blenches[10] gave my heart another youth,
> And worse essays prov'd thee my best of love.
> Now all is done, have what shall have no end,
> Mine appetite I never more will grind
> On newer proof, to try an older friend,
> A god in love, to whom I am confin'd.
> > Then give me welcome, next my heaven the best,
> > Even to thy pure and most most loving breast.

The first three lines would fit the situation of a fastidious person making himself a mountebank on the stage, but by

---

8. the fool's particolored dress   9. offended old friends by making new ones
10. glances aside

the time we have read through line 8 we feel that the behavior the speaker refers to must involve some kind of disloyalty in love. *Askaunce* means "with a sidelong glance, indifferently"; *blenches* means both "swervings away from constancy" and "blemishes." *Worse essays* means "experiments in what was inferior." The argument is that the speaker's infidelities have resulted in deeper love. . . .

THE PERSONA AS GUILTY

There is a comparison of the two offenses,[11] or rather of their effect upon the person offended, in Sonnet 120:

> That you were once unkind befriends me now,
> And for that sorrow which I then did feel
> Needs must I under my transgression bow,
> Unless my nerves were brass or hammered steel.
> For if you were by my unkindness shaken
> As I by yours, y'have pass'd a hell of time,
> And I, a tyrant, have no leisure taken
> To weigh how once I suffered in your crime.
> O that our night of woe might have rememb'red[12]
> My deepest sense, how hard true sorrow hits,
> And soon to you, as you to me then, tend'red
> The humble salve which wounded bosoms fits!
>   But that your trespass now becomes a fee,
>   Mine ransoms yours, and yours must ransom me.

The "I" is very frank about the extent of his guilt:

> To bitter sauces did I frame my feeding,
> And sick of welfare, found a kind of meetness[13]
> To be diseas'd ere that there was true needing.
>
> (118.6–8)

and again

> What potions I have drunk of Siren tears,
> Distill'd from limbecks[14] foul as hell within,
> Applying fears to hopes, and hopes to fears,
> Still losing when I saw myself to win!
>
> (119.1–4)

The identity of the poet's fault is left mysterious, as is the fault of the friend, but from its described effects and the imagery of food, disease, and wandering, one might well conclude that the offense was some kind of inconstancy. This is all the more apparent if we take the famous Sonnet 116 as an evocation of the opposite. The series 117–20 (or 121) is not, I think, a series of footnotes or attempts at parody of 116.

---

11. the friend's and the poet's   12. reminded   13. fitness   14. stills

THE PERSONA AS A CONSTANT LOVER

These sonnets, which discuss the many facets of the vice of inconstancy, have their implied opposite—constancy. This is defined, both negatively and positively, in 116. For purposes of comprehension it is better to read it *after* the sonnets on the fault. What is Love, and what is it not?

> Let me not to the marriage of true minds
> Admit impediments; love is not love
> Which alters when it alteration finds,
> Or bends with the remover to remove.[15]
> O no, it is an ever-fixëd mark
> That looks on tempests and is never shaken;
> It is the star to every wand'ring bark,
> Whose worth's unknown, although his highth be taken.
> Love's not Time's fool, though rosy lips and cheeks
> Within his bending sickle's compass come,
> Love alters not with his brief hours and weeks,
> But bears it out even to the edge of doom.
>   If this be error and upon me proved,
>   I never writ, nor no man ever loved.

This sonnet is justly a favorite. Its structure is clean and uncomplicated: three quatrains and a couplet, each quatrain beginning with a run-on line and ending with a strongly marked pause. The couplet rises to an almost defiant gesture, asserting again everything that has been said before. "Admit impediments" in line 2 invokes the marriage ceremony, and the tone and imagery of the first quatrain are rather formal and abstract. The second quatrain, with its images of a sea-mark unshaken by tempests and the Pole star with its navigational integrity, is more concrete yet highly romantic. The third quatrain, on the superiority of love to Time, evokes images like those in Hotspur's dying speech:

> But thoughts, the slaves of life, and life, time's fool,
> And time, that takes survey of all the world,
> Must have a stop.
>   (*1 Henry IV*, V, iv, 81–83)

The marriage of true minds is the subject. Douglas Hamer has traced the theme back to an anonymous fifth-century Arian, then to a homily in the form of *Matrimonium non facit coitus, sed voluntas,* "Marriage is not made by the coition of two bodies, but by the union of two minds!" He relates this, usefully, to the union of Othello and Desdemona (I, iii, 252–65). . . .

---

15. wishes to change when the loved one is inconstant

POEMS TO BE HEARD, NOT OVERHEARD

Whether in praise of the Fair Friend, or in complaint about his fault, or in justification of the poet's own shortcomings, the sonnets numbered 18–126 in the 1609 edition constitute an unrivaled masterwork. They are love poetry beyond what was considered love poetry by the Petrarchan sonneteers. Some are philosophical poems, meditations on the conflict between Time and ephemeral beauty, or between monuments of marble and immortal verse. Some are celebrations of the intimate relationship between the seasons of the year and human emotions. They are, often, ingenious exercises in wit—verbal, rhetorical, logical. They are not, I think, in any way poems meant to be "overheard." They speak, most of the time, to a *persona*, perhaps invented, perhaps derived in some way from an actual person. They are lyric poems, expressing mainly feelings that any capable reader can respond to as profound and true. But they are poems of the second voice, poems addressed to an audience of one or more, poems to be heard and mentally responded to. They are, for the most part, not soliloquies, or overheard poems. They derive some force from this fact. The persona of the hearer enables the reader to participate in the poem in a more active way than is possible for the overhearer. The poem is not quite dialogue but it is closer to dialogue than to soliloquy. This is the kind of poem that only a dramatist could write. Even in the compass of the sonnets, all the world's a stage.

The Sonnets Are Examples of Persuasive Rhetoric

David Parker

David Parker analyzes Shakespeare's sonnets as persuasive pieces, not statements about a subject. According to Parker, Shakespeare's sonnets are "great specimens of eloquence" in the Elizabethan tradition of rhetoric. Parker argues that Shakespeare's choice of verbs helps to create the graceful, tactful persuasive effect. He provides several examples to illustrate his point.

David Parker has taught at the University of Malaya in Malaysia and contributed articles to scholarly journals.

The poetic life of Shakespeare's sonnets is essentially a dramatic life. The temptation to discover for every piece of literature a "subject," something that it is "about," is understandable. Literature, like the sentences it is composed of, consists of words, and there seems to be no reason why we should not look for the subjects of literary works in the way we look for the subjects (logical rather than grammatical) of sentences. Most sentences, that is. It is easy to forget that it is only the majority of sentences, whose main verbs are in the indicative mood, that assert, that can be logically broken down into subject and predicate. Sentences whose main verbs are in the subjunctive mood, that are either imperative or interrogative, rarely assert; and when they do, they do so in odd ways. The imperative mood is particularly difficult. The sentence "Go away!" cannot be analyzed into subject and predicate, and to ask what it is about is strangely nonsensical.

It is profitable, at least temporarily, to consider Shakespeare's sonnets as other than statements. The way I recommend they be considered suggests that their mood is imper-

Excerpted from "Verbal Moods in Shakespeare's Sonnets" by David Parker, *Modern Language Quarterly*, vol. 30, no. 3 (September 1969), pp. 331–39. Copyright University of Washington, 1969. Reprinted with permission.

ative, in much the same way as did the old Elizabethan judgment of the sonnets as great specimens of eloquence, conceived not simply as good arguing, but as the effective use of
a rhetoric that persuades by means of logic, verbal trickery,
melody, the expression and deployment of strong feelings—
in fact, the whole range of mental experience and literary
technique the poet can muster. The heart of eloquence is not
assertion, the expression of fact, but demand, the expression
of will in such a way that the person addressed responds, or
at least feels guilty about not responding. . . .

SONNETS: THE ART OF POLITE PERSUASION

Nearly all the sonnets can be seen as elaborate disguises of
the imperative mood; and some, in the way they mix, balance, and play off against one another the different verbal
moods, demonstrate Shakespeare's sensitivity to the intricate
relations of these moods. The concept of the rhetorical question suggests that these moods are more flexible in their uses
than might at first appear, and the logical positivists of the
1930's, whether or not we agree with all their conclusions,
certainly demonstrated that statements, especially ones
about value, may perform more than an indicative function.

Sonnet 3 illustrates particularly well the flexibility of verbal mood and Shakespeare's sensitivity to it.

> Look in thy glass and tell the face thou viewest,
> Now is the time that face should form another,
> Whose fresh repair[1] if now thou not renewest,
> Thou dost beguile the world, unbless some mother.
> For where is she so fair whose uneared womb
> Disdains the tillage of thy husbandry?
> Or who is he so fond will be the tomb,
> Of this self-love to stop posterity?[2]
> Thou art thy mother's glass and she in thee
> Calls back the lovely April of her prime,
> So thou through windows of thine age shalt see,
> Despite of wrinkles this thy golden time.
> > But if thou live remembered not to be,[3]
> > Die single and thine image dies with thee.

The first quatrain, a single sentence, has two main verbs
in the imperative mood: "*Look* in thy glass and *tell*. . . ." The
poet is boldly making demands on the young man. But these
demands are softened and disguised by the shape and eva-

---

1. renewal   2. through sheer selfishness would not have a child and, thus, stop posterity   3. not to be remembered

sive circumlocution of the sentence. The poet's imperatives are got out of the way right at the beginning of the sentence and of the poem, and they are made acceptable by their insistence only on preliminary emblems of, or steps toward, what the poet wants: the boy has only to stand before a mirror and talk to himself. The demand is carried off with the sort of tactful daring that allows a man to bully his superior into doing something he knows he will not refuse.

The next important verb, "that face *should* form another," is in the subjunctive mood in order to express exhortation. *Should*, however, is such a common form that we hardly realize it is other than indicative. Used as a synonym of *ought*, it purports to be a straightforward statement about the established rules of behavior. . . .

SONNET 144—A SONNET WITH DOUBLE PERSUASION

In Shakespeare's Sonnet 144, the poet comments on the situation in which a dark woman has seduced a fair friend. The poet describes the event in language that suggests that the woman should be ashamed and the friend should reform.

Two loves I have, of comfort and despair,
Which like two spirits do suggest[1] me still.
The better angel is a man right fair,
The worser spirit a woman colour'd ill.
To win me soon to hell, my female evil
Tempteth my better angel from my side,
And would corrupt my saint to be a devil,
Wooing his purity with her foul pride.
And whether that my angel be turn'd fiend
Suspect I may, yet not directly tell;
But being both from me, both to each friend,
I guess one angel in another's hell.
     Yet this shall I ne'er know, but live in doubt,
     Till my bad angel fire my good one out.

1. tempt

But both strength and directness are rendered innocuous because the words are part of what, in indirect speech, the young man is supposed to say. This device disarmingly suggests that it is what any reasonable young man might say. In the following two lines there are three verbs:

Whose fresh repair if now thou not *renewest*,
Thou *dost beguile* the world, *unbless* some mother.

. . . Tact is maintained only if the words are supposed to be those of the young man.

Two rhetorical questions, apparently parallel, make up the second quatrain. Though interrogative in form, the first functions as a complimentary statement:

> For where is she so fair whose uneared womb
> Disdains the tillage of thy husbandry?

The roundabout form stops the flattery being too gross. The second question, however, behaves as a reproach, an accusatory statement:

> Or who is he so fond will be the tomb,
> Of this self-love to stop posterity?

It is the apparent parallel that makes it gentler. The young man, the poet hopes, will be too happy basking in the praise of rhetorical question one to notice the different intention of rhetorical question two other than by modifying, almost without noticing it, his attitudes and behavior, so as to avoid the implied charge. Question two, we may say, functions not only as a statement, but as a very attenuated imperative.

The third quatrain is full of direct indicatives that strike the reader as bold and optimistic. The one in line 11 is the most compelling:

> So thou through windows of thine age *shalt* see,
> Despite of wrinkles this thy golden time.

. . . The young man is virtually challenged not to fulfill such a sunny prophecy.

The couplet contains an unusual and intriguing ambiguity of mood:

> But if thou live remembered not to be,
> Die single and thine image dies with thee.

. . . The caesura after *single* would be very heavy indeed—a deep sigh of dejection, as it were—and the final words, "and thine image dies with thee," an afterthought uttered with relentless, heartbreaking logic. This final melancholy contemplation of the evaporation of the young man's beauty as an achieved fact—the verb is in the present indicative—acts only as the gentlest of warnings, and its static brooding quality is the last disguise assumed by the continuous series of imperatives the poem covertly presses.

Sonnet 3 is perhaps not among the finest of the sonnets, but it aptly illustrates the variety and subtlety of Shakespeare's use of verbal moods and the essentially suasive quality of the sonnets. The early group on "breed" are often seen, with their clearly stated aim, as a special category, but among the 154 sonnets there are scarcely any that could be conclusively denied a suasive intention.

SONNETS THAT INSTRUCT AND REFORM

The terrible "lust in action" sonnet (129) is usually understood as a piece of self-hatred. The verbs are all outraged, dogmatic indicatives. But in the exhausted, embittered, and moralizing couplet, an intention emerges.

> All this the world well knows yet none knows well,
> To shun the heaven that leads men to this hell.

General statements about human weakness rarely lack prescriptive force, and this is no exception. After the frenzy of the first twelve lines, the jogtrot rhythm and truistic sentiment of the couplet establish it as a maxim, the self-evident truth and neglect of which make it the cause of disenchantment that is itself instructive. Whether Shakespeare is trying to instruct himself or another is hardly important. . . .

Sonnet 144 ("Two loves I have of comfort and despair") is probably meant to serve a double function: to make the woman writhe, the young man blush and reform. Sonnet 130 ("My mistress' eyes are nothing like the sun") pretends to be an announcement of disillusionment, but turns into a compliment, changing its tone rather sooner than is usually realized, at the third quatrain:

> I love to hear her speak, yet well I know,
> That music hath a far more pleasing sound:
> I grant I never saw a goddess go,
> My mistress when she walks treads on the ground.
>> And yet by heaven I think my love as rare,
>> As any she belied with false compare.

With "I love to hear her speak," Shakespeare allows the reader to glimpse his hand. The qualification reveals only sturdy common sense, music being admired chiefly because its sound is more pleasing than that of speech. His impatience with nonsense is continued in line 11, "I grant I never saw a goddess go," which issues a challenge to the hyperbolists to state what basis in experience their similes have. The next line is effectively ambivalent. Compared to the means of locomotion we imagine for goddesses, walking on the ground may seem a disadvantage, but having "both feet on the ground" is a virtue that befits the mistress of a poet who will stand no nonsense. The couplet dispenses with the apparatus of hyperbolic rhetoric at the same time that it compliments the woman by denying its adequacy to do her justice.

The sonnet, in fact, operates as a cathartic compliment, exploiting the relief felt in starting afresh by discarding the lumber of tradition, propriety, and tact. As a compliment it is a statement about value: consequently, under cover of the indicative mood, it demands a response—in this case a change or intensification of attitudes toward the speaker. . . .

DEMAND DISGUISED BY TACT AND ELOQUENCE

The sense of extreme tension, of delicate but ambiguous judgment and impassioned casuistry,[4] that characterizes nearly all the sonnets derives very largely from the enormous effort put into staying tactful, an effort simply to disguise the imperative mood, an effort that is the heart of eloquence. . . .

It is possible at one level of interpretation to be content with assuming that [Shakespeare] adopted the postures such beliefs entailed in order to influence those to whom his sonnets were addressed. Shakespeare was certainly in some sense a poet of ideas and theories, but he was no less a poet of men and women, and it is difficult not to believe that the relationships suggested in the sonnets were as vivid and active as those shown in the plays.

4. the practice of misleading by subtle reasoning

The Use of Sound in Shakespeare's Sonnets

Barbara Herrnstein Smith

Barbara Herrnstein Smith argues that sound—the accented words making the rhythm and the combinations of vowels and consonants making the music—is as important to Shakespeare's style as his figurative language, images, and metaphors. Shakespeare used already developed techniques, Smith says, but he used them more effectively. Poets had discovered that the most natural meter for poetry in English is iambic, a two-syllable unit with the second syllable accented (marked ˘ ´). Strict iambic meter can sound artificial and mechanical, but Shakespeare made the meter sound natural. Smith argues that, in addition to his skillful way with meter, Shakespeare expertly put words together to make musical sounds with combinations and repetitions of vowel and consonant sounds. In a couplet from Sonnet 18, Smith notes seven long vowel sounds in *so, breathe, eyes, see, so, life,* and *thee.* In an excerpt from Sonnet 55, the sounds of the consonants *n*, *p*, and *l* are each repeated.

Barbara Herrnstein Smith has taught English at Brandeis University in Waltham, Massachusetts, at Bennington College in Vermont, and is now at Duke University in Durham, North Carolina. She has published two books on Shakespeare's sonnets as well as other works of poetry criticism and literary history.

The *Sonnets* are as various in other aspects of style as they are in their structure, and the most secure generalization one can make in this regard is that generalizations are almost impossible to make. . . .

Shakespeare's most distinctive and effective figures cannot be analyzed [logically], as certain critics, wielding the metaphysical ax they seek to grind, have pointed out. The grammar is ungrammatical, they protest—the logic is illogical, the metaphors are mixed, nothing makes sense. It depends, however, upon what sort of sense one expects to be made. It is true that the figurative texture of Shakespeare's poetry is often so thickly woven that it is impossible to trace or sort out the threads. . . .

THE STRUCTURE OF SOUNDS

No description of Shakespeare's style can begin and end only with his figures. Hardly less important, for example, is the meter or general structure of sounds in his poetry.

SHAKESPEARE'S NATURAL-SOUNDING SPEECH

Like other poets of his time, Shakespeare wrote lines of regularly accented syllables, but he managed to make the meter sound like natural speech. Sonnet 129, which follows, has been scanned to show how Shakespeare varied its otherwise regular pattern in lines 4, 9, and 10.

The expense of spirit in a waste of shame
Is lust in action, and till action, lust
Is perjured, murderous, bloody, full of blame,
Savage, extreme, rude, cruel, not to trust,
Enjoyed no sooner but despised straight,   5
Past reason hunted, and no sooner had,
Past reason hated, as a swallowed bait,
On purpose laid to make the taker mad.
Mad in pursuit, and in possession so,
Had, having, and in quest to have, extreme,   10
A bliss in proof, and proved, a very woe.
Before, a joy proposed, behind, a dream.
    All this the world well knows, yet none knows well
    To shun the Heaven that leads men to this Hell.

Shakespeare and his immediate contemporaries were the heirs of a century of experimentation with the poetic resources of the English language. The sixteenth century had opened with meter in a state of almost barbaric confusion, and closed with it in a state of subtle sophistication; and what had been discovered and perfected in the interim were techniques that dominated English poetry until our own time. Shakespeare was hardly the first English poet to mas-

ter the basic accentual-syllabic line so that it neither dis-
torted the natural emphasis of speech nor maintained its
form through a thumping mechanical regularity. Nevertheless, it may be doubted whether any other poet surpassed
him in managing that line with the flexibility and expres-
siveness these passages illustrate:

> Then hate me when thou wilt—if ever, now,
> Now while the world is bent my deeds to cross ...   (90)

> Th' expense of spirit in a waste of shame
> Is lust in action, and, till action, lust
> Is perjured, murd'rous, bloody, full of blame,
> Savage, extreme, rude, cruel, not to trust ...   (129)

> How can it? O, how can love's eye be true,
> That is so vexed with watching and with tears?   (148)

> Alas, 'tis true, I have gone here and there
> And made myself a motley to the view,
> Gored mine own thoughts, sold cheap what is most dear,
> Made old offenses of affections new.   (110)

Shakespeare also mastered, to a degree matched by none
of his contemporaries and by few poets since, the essentially
sensuous or, as we say, "musical" potentialities of the language. The mastery is not, of course, a matter of how many
alliterated syllables one can crowd into one line, but the
more subtle and complex distributions and patterns of phonetic elements which, operating in conjunction with internal rhythm, produce "the true concord of well-tuned
sounds" (8) that we hear in these lines:

> So long as men can breathe or eyes can see,
> So long lives this, and this gives life to thee.   (18)

> Not marble nor the gilded monuments
> Of princes shall outlive this powerful rhyme ...   (55)

> No longer mourn for me, when I am dead,
> Than you shall hear the surly sullen bell
> Give warning to the world that I am fled
> From this vile world, with vildest worms to dwell.   (71)

It is true that certain of Shakespeare's *Sonnets* may remind us of Spenser and the Petrarchan style of other Elizabethan poets, that others will remind us of Donne and the
seventeenth-century metaphysical amorists, and yet others
of Ralegh and a certain native, pre-Elizabethan style. In each
case, however, the pull of Shakespeare's individual poetic
personality and imagination—his "style" in the broadest
sense—is evident, and not many of the sonnets could be mis-

taken for the work of any other poet. Shakespeare had no immediate followers: there was no Shakespearean movement or trend or school of poetry. His greatness was, like Milton's, essentially inimitable. Style, as such, cannot be imitated; only mannerisms can, and Shakespeare's style was not a matter of mannerisms. When we seek to describe or define it fully, we find that at some point we must begin to speak not only of characteristic techniques, but of characteristic themes and tones, and perhaps what we might call temperament. Shakespeare's style was a function of the way he reacted to the world, the way he perceived and connected his own experiences—ways that were, finally, so extraordinary, that we know we shall not look upon his like again.

CHAPTER 3

Themes in the Sonnets

READINGS ON
THE SONNETS

Shakespeare's Sonnets Are the World's Greatest Love Poems

John Dover Wilson

Quoting modern critics, John Dover Wilson argues that Shakespeare's sonnets are above all great love poetry. Wilson suggests that the reader get beyond the particulars of biography and publication to grasp the essence of the sonnets' expression of universal love, or else the meaning of the sonnets will be, according to Wilson, like the shadows in Greek philosopher Plato's parable of the cave—distortions of reality.

John Dover Wilson, a prominent Shakespearean scholar and author, was also the editor of *The New Shakespeare*, an annotated and revised edition of the collected works acclaimed worldwide. Wilson taught at the University of Helsingfors, Finland; the University of London; and the University of Edinburgh.

Sir Walter Raleigh, who wrote the most human short life of William Shakespeare that we possess, began his section on the *Sonnets* as follows: 'There are many footprints around the cave of this mystery, none of them pointing in the outward direction. No one has ever attempted a solution of the problem without leaving a book behind him; and the shrine of Shakespeare is thickly hung with these votive offerings, all withered and dusty'. Raleigh's cave of mystery calls another to mind, Plato's cave of illusion in which the human race sit chained with their backs to the sun without, and are condemned to accept the passing shadows on the wall before them for the truth—the real truth being only revealed to the few who are able to break their bonds and turn to face the light of day. Absorbed in our own attempts to solve the biographical puzzles that the individual sonnets offer us, we remain blind to the sun that casts these shadows but gives

Excerpted from *An Introduction to the Sonnets of Shakespeare: For the Use of Historians and Others* by J. Dover Wilson (New York: Cambridge University Press, 1963).

WILLIAM BLAKE'S POEM ON LOVE

Critic C.S. Lewis, quoted by John Dover Wilson, compares Shakespeare's giving kind of love to the clod of clay, the first image in William Blake's poem "The Clod and the Pebble." In Blake's poem, reprinted below, the clod of clay symbolizes selfless love and the pebble symbolizes selfish love.

"Love seeketh not Itself to please,
Nor for itself hath any care;
But for another gives its ease,
And builds a Heaven in Hell's despair."

    So sang a little Clod of Clay,
    Trodden with the cattle's feet;
    But a Pebble of the brook,
    Warbled out these metres meet:

"Love seeketh only Self to please,
To bind another to its delight,
Joys in another's loss of ease,
And builds a Hell in Heaven's despite."

meaning to the whole. Begin by seeing that meaning and recognizing the whole as the greatest love-poem in the language, and the mystery of the detail becomes so unimportant as to fade away.

SHAKESPEARE'S MODESTY

That this is the right approach to an understanding apparently so obvious and so natural, has in point of fact only quite recently been realised; and realised independently and almost simultaneously by two critics, both driven by a wide study of the love-poetry of the Renaissance to admit the uniqueness of Shakespeare's. 'There is no parallel', writes J.W. Lever in a sensitive and learned book on *The Elizabethan Love-Sonnet*, 'in the whole corpus of Renaissance poetry for Shakespeare's sustained exploration of the theme of friendship through more than 120 sonnets'. More significant still is what he calls the Poet's 'extreme capacity for self-effacement' and emphasises as not just an echo of the conventional sonnet lover's avowed humility. As he writes:[1]

> Sidney had always his Protestant conscience and the dignity
> of his rank for ultimate solace; Spenser, regarding courtship

1. about other poets

as a preliminary to the sacrament of marriage and the subordination of wife to husband, had stooped to conquer. Even Petrarch had sacrificed himself on the altar of love with a certain hauteur[2]—*E voglio anzi un sepolcro bello e bianco.*[3] But the self-effacement of Shakespeare as poet of the sonnets is total and unreserved. He has no place in nature or society save that accorded him by the Friend. He is in the autumn of his years, 'lame, poor, and despised', 'in disgrace with fortune and men's eyes'. . . . He envies this man's art and that man's scope. Far from planning, like Petrarch, a memorial of white marble to commemorate his love, he pleads to be left forgotten and unmourned, lest the world should mock the man who once befriended him:

> No longer mourn for me when I am dead
> Than you shall hear the surly sullen bell[4]
> Give warning to the world that I am fled
> From this vile world, with vilest worms to dwell:
> Nay, if you read this line, remember not
> The hand that writ it . . .   (71)

THE SONNETS EXPRESS UNIVERSAL LOVE

C.S. Lewis, the other critic I must quote, proclaims the *Sonnets* not only as unique in the period of the Renaissance but as the supreme love-poetry of the world.

He begins by disposing of the 'cave of mystery' in these terms:

> The difficulty which faces us if we try to read the sequence like a novel is that the precise mode of love which the poet declares for the man remains obscure. His language is too lover-like for that of ordinary male friendship, and though the claims of friendship are sometimes put very high in, say, the *Arcadia*, I have found no real parallel to such language between friends in sixteenth-century literature. Yet, on the other hand, this does not seem to be the poetry of full-blown pederasty.[5] Shakespeare, and indeed Shakespeare's age, did nothing by halves. If he had intended in these sonnets to be the poet of pederasty, I think he would have left us in no doubt; the lovely παιδικά,[6] attended by a whole train of mythological perversities, would have blazed across the page. The incessant demand that the man should marry and found a family would seem to be inconsistent (or so I suppose—it is a question for psychologists) with a real homosexual passion. It is not even very obviously consistent with sexual friendship. It is indeed hard to think of any real situation in which it would be natural. What man in the whole world, except a father or a potential father-in-law, cares whether any other

2. arrogance   3. Indeed, he is longing for a sepulcher beautiful and white   4. a bell tolled at the moment of a person's death   5. a sexual relationship between a man and a boy   6. *paidika*, songs to or about a beloved boy

man gets married? Thus the emotion expressed in the *Sonnets* refuses to fit into our pigeon-holes.

Such is the effect of individual sonnets. But when we read the whole sequence through at a sitting (as we ought surely to do) we have a different experience. From its total plot, however ambiguous, however particular, there emerges something not indeed common or general, like the love expressed in many individual sonnets, but yet, in a higher way, universal. The main contrast in the *Sonnets* is between the two loves, that 'of comfort' and that 'of despair'. The love 'of despair' demands all; the love 'of comfort' asks, and perhaps receives, nothing. Thus the whole sequence becomes an expanded version of Blake's *The Clod and the Pebble*. And so it comes about that, however the whole thing began—in perversion, in convention, even (who knows?) in fiction—Shakespeare, celebrating the 'Clod' as no man has celebrated it before or since, ends by expressing simply love, the quintessence of all loves whether erotic, parental, filial, amicable or feudal. Thus from extreme particularity there is a road to the highest universality. The love is, in the end, so simply and entirely love that our *cadres*[7] are thrown away and we cease to ask what kind. However it may have been with Shakespeare in his daily life, the greatest of the sonnets are written from a region in which love abandons all claims and flowers into charity; after that it makes little odds what the root was like. They open a new world of love-poetry: as new as Dante's and Petrarch's had been in their day. These had of course expressed humility, but it had been the humility of Eros, hungry to receive; kneeling, but kneeling to ask. They and their great successor Patmore[8] sing a dutiful and submissive, but hardly a giving, love. They could have written, almost too easily, 'Being your slave, what should I do but tend?'; they could hardly have written, 'I may not evermore acknowledge thee', or 'No longer mourn', or 'Although thou steal thee all my poverty'. The self-abnegation,[9] the 'naughting', in the *Sonnets* never rings false. This patience, this anxiety (more like a parent's than a lover's) to find excuse for the beloved, this clear-sighted and wholly unembittered resignation, this transference of the whole self into another self without the demand for a return, have hardly a precedent in profane literature. In certain senses of the word 'love', Shakespeare is not so much our best as our only love poet.

THE POET AND THE PATRON

There is nothing a mere editor can add to that except to quote what Keats tells us about the poet.

---

7. frameworks and definitions   8. Coventry Kersey Dighton, who published *The Unknown Eros* in 1877   9. giving up of the self for others

> A Poet is the most unpoetical thing in existence; because he
> has no identity—he is continually informing and filling some
> other Body—the Sun, the Moon, the Sea and Men and Women
> who as Creatures of impulse are poetical and have about
> them an unchangeable attribute—the poet has none; no iden-
> tity—he is certainly the most unpoetical of all God's creatures.

As a dramatic poet, Shakespeare has no identity; as a man
and a lover he is as selfless and humble as the clod of clay
in Blake's poem 'trodden with the cattle's feet'.

Thus the *Sonnets* are for all time. Yet their poet, being
human, was of an age, and in order that the modern reader
may not misunderstand the homage offered, I shall have to
remind him at times in many of the observations that follow
of certain Elizabethan conventions and modes of expression.
There is, however, one convention of sonnet-writers which
may be set down here in the words of T.G. Tucker, in one of
the best editions of the *Sonnets:*

> Shakespeare was the poet in 'service' or 'vassalage'[10] to his
> 'lord', and in the recognised manner of sonneteers, supposed
> himself bound to write piece after piece to the beloved with a
> certain continuity of production and with as much variety of
> 'invention' as possible upon his adopted theme. Any inter-
> mission of greater length than usual, any omission to keep up
> the regular supply of offerings at the altar, would call for self-
> reproach and apology; it would even supply the poet with
> matter for the next effort.

And there readers who have like Lewis chosen the better
part of enjoying the *Sonnets* as the greatest love-poetry in the
world and asking no further questions, may well shut this
introduction and pass directly on to Shakespeare himself.

10. in service to another

Shakespeare's Sonnets Portray a Maturing Love

Edward Dowden

Edward Dowden assumes that Shakespeare's sonnets reveal the mind and soul of their author, but not his particular activities and experiences. Dowden asserts that Shakespeare displays a sensitive, strong nature whose knowledge of love develops in phases. The early sonnets of the first phase express ideal, naive love. The middle sonnets of the second phase portray various facets of love: time's toll on love, loss of love, the misery of loving in the wrong way, and being wronged by a loved one. In the final phase, Shakespeare remains committed to love despite its sorrows and disappointments. In short, Dowden shows that Shakespeare exposes his warm and gracious heart while keeping his own experiences hidden.

During the late nineteenth century, Edward Dowden was professor of English literature in the University of Dublin and vice president of the New Shakespeare Society.

To understand in all essentials the history of Shakspere's character and Shakspere's art, we have obtained what is absolutely necessary when we have made out the succession, not of Shakspere's plays, but of Shakspere's chief visions of truth, his most intense moments of inspiration, his greater discoveries about human life.

In the history of every artist and of every man there are periods of quickened existence, when spiritual discovery is made without an effort, and attainment becomes easy and almost involuntary. One does not seek for truth, but rather is sought for by truth, and found; one does not construct beautiful imaginings, but beauty itself haunts and startles and

Excerpted from *Shakespere: A Critical Study of His Mind and Art* by Edward Dowden (New York: Harper & Bros., 1880).

waylays. These periods may be arrived at through prolonged moral conflict and victory, or through some sudden revelation of joy, or through supreme anguish and renouncement. Such epochs of spiritual discovery lie behind the art of the artist, it may be immediately, or it may be remotely, and out of these it springs. . . .

SONNETS 144 AND 146 SYMBOLIZE THE CENTRAL POINT OF THE SERIES

In Of Comfort and Despair: Shakespeare's Sonnet Sequence, *Robert W. Witt cites Sonnets 144 and 146 as companion poems that clarify Shakespeare's philosophy of love, a philosophy based on the theory of Greek philosopher Plato.*

Sonnet 146 not only serves as an excellent companion piece to 144 but together they serve as the conclusion of this Series as well as the entire Sequence. Sonnet 144 is a key poem because it makes clear that the man represents spiritual love and hence the soul and the woman sensual love and hence the body. Sonnet 146 then makes clear that the soul after all is of far more importance than the body and that it is to be nourished while the body is denied. This, of course, is the central point of the neo-Platonic theory of love. Reasonable love while denying the body develops the soul and leads it to sovereign happiness. Sensual love while satisfying the body destroys the soul and causes man to become beast-like. This is the point which the Sequence dramatizes.

Were there in the life of Shakspere certain events which compelled him to a bitter yet precious gain of experience in the matter of the wrongs of man to man, and from which he procured instruction in the difficult art of bearing one's self justly towards one's wrongers? If the *Sonnets* of Shakspere, written many years before the close of Shakspere's career as dramatist, be autobiographical, we may perhaps discover the sorrow which first roused his heart and imagination to their long inquisition of evil and grief, and which, sinking down into his great soul, and remaining there until all bitterness had passed away, bore fruit in the most mature of Shakspere's writings, distinguished as these are by serene pathetic strength and stern yet tender beauty.

The *Sonnets* of Shakspere were probably written during those years when, as dramatist, he was engaged upon the substantial material of English history, and when he was ac-

cumulating those resources which were to make him a
wealthy burgher¹ of Stratford. This practical, successful
man, who had now arrived at middle age, and was growing
rich; who had never found delight, as . . . other wild livers
had, in the flimsy idealism of knocking his head against the
solid laws of the world—was yet not altogether that self-
possessed, cheerful, prudent person who has stood with
some writers for the veritable Shakspere. In the *Sonnets* we
recognize three things: that Shakspere was capable of measureless personal devotion; that he was tenderly sensitive—
sensitive, above all, to every diminution or alteration of that
love his heart so eagerly craved; and that when wronged, although he suffered anguish, he transcended his private injury, and learned to forgive. . . .

SHAKSPERE: SENSITIVE, UNTESTED, SPIRITED

What no reader will find anywhere in the plays or poems of
Shakspere is a cold-blooded, hard, or selfish line; all is
warm, sensitive, vital, radiant with delight, or athrill with
pain. And what we may dare to affirm of Shakspere's life is,
that whatever its sins may have been, they were not hard,
selfish, deliberate, cold-blooded sins. The errors of his heart
originated in his sensitiveness, in his imagination (not at
first inured to the harness of fidelity to the fact), in his quick
consciousness of existence, and in the self-abandoning devotion of his heart. There are some noble lines by Chapman²
which he pictures to himself the life of great energy, enthu-
siasms, and passions which forever stands upon the edge of
utmost danger, and yet forever remains in absolute security:

> Give me the spirit that on this life's rough sea
> Loves to have his sails filled with a lusty wind
> Even till his sail-yards tremble, his masts crack,
> And his rapt ship run on her side so low
> That she drinks water, and her keel ploughs air;
> There is no danger to a man that knows
> What life and death is—there's not any law
> Exceeds his knowledge; neither is it lawful
> That he should stoop to any other law.³

Such a master-spirit, pressing forward under strained
canvas, was Shakspere. If the ship dipped and drank water,
she rose again; and, at length, we behold her within view of

---

1. a middle-class citizen   2. poet and playwright George   3. from *The Conspiracy and
Tragedy of Byron*, Act III, Sc. 1

her haven, sailing under a large, calm wind, not without to-
kens of stress of weather, but, if battered, yet unbroken by
the waves. It is to dull, lethargic natures that a moral acci-
dent is fatal, because they are tending nowhither, and lack
energy and momentum to right themselves again. To say
anything against decent lethargic vices and timid virtues,
anything to the advantage of the strenuous life of bold action
and eager emotion, which necessarily incurs risks, and
sometimes suffers, is, we shall be told, "dangerous." Well,
then, be it so; it is dangerous.

The Shakspere whom we discern in the *Sonnets* had certainly not attained the broad mastery of life which the Stratford bust asserts to have been Shakspere's in his closing
years. Life had been found good by him who owned those
lips, and whose spirit declares itself in the massive animation
of the total outlook of that face.[4] When the greater number of
these *Sonnets* were written, Shakspere could have understood Romeo; he could have understood Hamlet; he could
not have conceived Duke Prospero.[5] Under the joyous exte-
rior of those days lay a craving, sensitive, unsatisfied heart,
which had not entire possession of itself, which could mis-
place its affections, and resort to all those pathetic frauds by
which misplaced affections strive to conceal an error from
themselves. The friend in whose personality Shakspere
found a source of measureless delight—high-born, beautiful,
young, clever, accomplished, ardent—wronged him. The
woman from whom Shakspere for a time received a joyous
quickening of his life, which was half pain—a woman of
stained character, and the reverse of beautiful, but a strong
nature, intellectual, a lover of art, and possessed of curious
magnetic attraction, with her dark eyes, which illuminated a
pale face—wronged him also. Shakspere bitterly felt the
wrong—felt most bitterly the wrong which was least to be expected, that of his friend. It has been held to be an additional
baseness that Shakspere could forgive, that he could rescue
himself from indignant resentment, and adjust his nature to
the altered circumstances. Possibly Shakspere may not have
subscribed to all the items in the code of honor; he may not
have regarded as inviolable the prohibited degrees of for-

4. This is the more remarkable, because the original of the bust was almost certainly
a mask taken after death; and the bust betrays the presence of physical death, over
which, however, life triumphs. The bust is erected in the Church of the Holy Trinity at
Stratford-on-Avon, overlooking Shakespeare's grave. 5. of *The Tempest*

giveness. He may have seen that the wrong done to him was human, natural, almost inevitable. He certainly saw that the chief wrong was not that done to him, but committed by his friend against his own better nature. Delivering his heart from the prepossessions of wounded personal feeling, and looking at the circumstances as they actually were, he may have found it very natural and necessary not to banish from his heart the man he loved. However this may have been, his own sanity and strength, and the purity of his work as artist, depended on his ultimately delivering his soul from all bitterness. Besides, life was not exhausted. The ship righted itself, and went ploughing forward across a broad sea. Shakspere found ever more and more in life to afford adequate sustenance for man's highest needs of intellect and of heart. Life became ever more encircled with presences of beauty, of goodness, and of terror; and Shakspere's fortitude of heart increased. Nevertheless, such experiences as those recorded in the *Sonnets* could not pass out of his life, and in the imaginative recurrence of past moods might at any subsequent time become motives of his art. Passion had been purified; and at last the truth of things stood out clear and calm.

Shakspere Gains Maturity and Strength Through Sorrow

The *Sonnets* tell more of Shakspere's sensitiveness than of Shakspere's strength. In the earlier poems of the collection, his delight in human beauty, intellect, grace, expresses itself with endless variation. Nothing seems to him more admirable than manhood. But this joy is controlled and saddened by a sense of the transitoriness of all things, the ruin of time, the inevitable progress of decay. The love expressed in the early *Sonnets* is love which has known no sorrow, no change, no wrong; it is an ecstasy which the sensitive heart is as yet unable to control:

> As an unperfect actor on the stage
> Who with his fear is put beside his part,
> Or some fierce thing replete with too much rage,
> Whose strength's abundance weakens his own heart,
> So I, for fear of trust, forget to say
> The perfect ceremony of love's rite,
> And in mine own love's strength seem to decay,
> O'ercharged with burden of mine own love's might.
>
> (Sonnet 23, ll. 1–8)

The prudent and sober Shakspere—was it he who bore this

burden of too much love, he whose heart was made weak by the abundance of its strength? He cannot sleep; he lies awake, haunted in the darkness by the face that is dear to him. He falls into sudden moods of despondency, when his own gifts seem narrow and of little worth; when his poems, which yield him his keenest enjoyment, seem wretchedly remote from what he had dreamed, and, in the midst of his depression, he almost despises himself because he is depressed:

> Wishing me like to one more rich in hope,
> Featured like him, like him with friends possess'd,
> Desiring this man's art and that man's scope,
> With what I most enjoy contented least.   (Sonnet 29, ll. 5–8)

He weeps for the loss of precious friends, for "love's long-since-cancelled woe;" but out of all these clouds and damps the thought of one human soul, which he believes beautiful, can deliver him:

> Haply I think on thee, and then my state,
> Like to the lark at break of day arising
> From sullen earth, sings hymns at heaven's gate.
> (Sonnet 29, ll. 10–12)

Then comes the bitter discovery—a change in love that had seemed to be made for eternity; coldness, estrangement, wrongs upon both sides; and, at the same time, external trials and troubles arise, and the injurious life of actor and playwright—injurious to the delicate harmony and purity of the poet's nature—becomes more irksome:

> And almost thence my nature is subdued
> To what it works in, like the dyer's hand.
> (Sonnet 111, ll. 6–7)

He pathetically begs, not now for love, but for pity. Yet at the worst, and through all suffering, he believes in love:

> Let me not to the marriage of true minds
> Admit impediments. Love is not love
> Which alters when it alteration finds.   (Sonnet 116, ll. 1–3)

It can accept its object even though imperfect, and still love on. It is not, in the common acceptation of the word, prudential—but the *infinite* prudence of the heart is indeed no other than love:

> It fears not Policy, that heretic
> Which works on leases of short-number'd hours,
> But all alone stands hugely politic,
> That it nor glows with heat, nor drowns with showers.
> (Sonnet 124, ll. 9–12)

He has learned his lesson; his romantic attachment, which attributed an impossible perfection to his friend, has become the stronger love which accepts his friend and knows the fact; knows the fact of frailty and imperfection; knows also the greater and infinitely precious fact of central and sur-viving loyalty and goodness: and this new love is better than the old, because more real:

> O benefit of ill! now I find true
> That better is by evil still made better;
> And ruin'd love, when it is built anew,
> Grows fairer than at first, more strong, far greater.
> (Sonnet 119, ll. 9–12)

And thus he possesses his soul once more; he "returns to his content."

Such, briefly and imperfectly hinted, is the spirit of Shakspere's *Sonnets*. A great living poet, who has dedicated to the subject of friendship one division of his collected works, has written these words:

> Recorders ages hence?
> Come, I will take you down underneath this impassive
>   exterior—I will tell you what to say of me;
> Publish my name, and hang up my picture as that of the
>   tenderest lover.

And elsewhere, of these Calamus poems,[6] the poems of ten-der and hardy friendship, he says,

> Here the frailest leaves of me, and yet my strongest-lasting:
> Here I shade and hide my thoughts—I myself do not expose them,
> And yet they expose me more than all my other poems.

These words of Whitman may be taken as a motto of the *Sonnets* of Shakspere. In these poems Shakspere has hidden himself, and is exposed.

---

6. a section of American poet Walt Whitman's *Leaves of Grass*

The Dark Lady Sonnets Explore Passion and Its Effects

Edward Hubler

Edward Hubler analyzes Shakespeare's treatment of passion in the sonnets addressed to a dark lady. Unlike the chaste, blond beauty in traditional Elizabethan sonnets, Shakespeare's woman is dark, both in appearance and deed. Hubler traces the changes in the poet's attitude toward this woman. In a humorous tone, the poet first expresses his love in spite of her lack of beauty. His attitude shifts to regret and remorse when he realizes her faults and his inability to detach himself from the promiscuous woman. Hubler ends his analysis with Sonnet 146, in which the poet sees death as the way to save his soul.

Edward Hubler taught at the University of Rochester in New York and Princeton University, and he was a Fulbright professor at the Universities of Bordeaux and Toulouse in France. He published numerous works on Shakespeare's plays and the sonnets.

In one of his plays Yeats[1] asks, "If pleasure and remorse must both be there, which is the greater?" It is a question quite central to a consideration of Shakespeare's dark lady, for the sonnets devoted to her tell of an amour which began in pleasure and ended in moral loathing. . . .

SHAKESPEARE'S LADY UNLIKE TRADITIONAL SONNET BEAUTY

There is nothing like the woman of Shakespeare's sonnets in all the sonnet literature of the Renaissance. The ladies of the sonnet tradition were idealizations; Shakespeare's heroine represents neither the traditional ideal nor his. The Eliza-

---

1. Irish writer William Butler

Excerpted from *The Sense of Shakespeare's Sonnets* by Edward Hubler (Princeton, NJ: Princeton University Press, 1952).

bethan ideal of beauty was blonde; Shakespeare's heroine, if
we may call her that, was dark, and the blackness of her hair
and eyes and heart is so heavily stressed that she has come
to be known as "the dark lady." He insists upon her darkness—first the darkness of her beauty, and later the darkness
of her deeds. But from the beginning, even when his passion
for her was untouched by regret, his praise of her beauty was
marked by ambivalence. It was perhaps the dominance of
the traditional and popular ideal which made him distrust
the dictates of his senses. He opens the series with

> In the old age black was not counted fair,
> Or if it were, it bore not beauty's name.   (Sonnet 127)

. . . Sometimes the poet tells her that her eyes are black because they know of her disdain for him, that they have put
on mourning in recognition of his bondage to her. Whatever
their context, Shakespeare's compliments are always shad-
owed by his awareness of a discrepancy between the ideal
and the fact, although there were times when the fact did not
seem to matter:

> My mistress' eyes are nothing like the sun;
> Coral is far more red than her lips' red:
> If snow be white, why then her breasts are dun;
> If hairs be wires, black wires grow on her head.
> I have seen roses damask'd[2] red and white,
> But no such roses see I in her cheeks;
> And in some perfumes is there more delight
> Than in the breath that from my mistress reeks.
> I love to hear her speak, yet well I know
> That music hath a far more pleasing sound:
> I grant I never saw a goddess go;
> My mistress, when she walks, treads on the ground:
> > And yet, by heaven, I think my love as rare
> > As any she belied with false compare.   (Sonnet 130)

Aware of the ideal, he here declares himself in favor of al-
loyed reality. He does not say that he loves her in spite of her
faults; he loves her faults and all.

Considered in itself, the sonnet is pure comedy, at least by
Meredith's[3] standard, which required that the possessor of
the comic spirit see the ridiculous in those he loved without
loving them less. The spirit of "My mistress' eyes" is the
spirit in which Dogberry, Falstaff,[4] and the whole world of
lovable imperfections were created. In this sense the poem

---

2. variegated pink and white   3. English writer George   4. flawed but likeable Shakespearean characters

is the essence of comedy. But if the poem is read in the light of the sonnet tradition, it is also satire. If we would appreciate Shakespeare's complexity, we must realize that this is not an *either/or* matter. The sonnet is satire or comedy or both, depending on what the reader brings to it. The sonnet contains them both, the only variable being the reader's ability to see. In this respect the sonnet is like the greater part of Shakespeare's work—hardly ever simple, hardly ever exhausted at one level of meaning. The reader of Shakespeare's day who had the slightest acquaintance with modern poetry could not have missed the satire on the heroine of the sonnet tradition. . . .

THE DARK LADY SONNETS AS PARODIES

In Shakespeare's Sugared Sonnets, *Katherine M. Wilson analyzes the dark lady sonnets as parodies, or humorous imitations, of traditional Elizabethan sonnets. Shakespeare's mockserious tone fools many readers.*

In his sonnets on the lady, Shakespeare has been writing in plain speech of ugly prose facts, treating the whole thing with mock seriousness as a man dealing with facts must, and simulated it so well that many of his readers, even although he has surprised them, have taken it all for truth. But he ends with two sonnets of sugared myth, which sound quite unreal and artificial after his common-sensical down to hell treatment of the sonnet tradition.

The hopelessness of Shakespeare's love is another matter. He despairs of his lady because there is no loyalty in her. She is, he remarks in nautical terms, "the bay where all men ride.". . .

The lady of the sonnet tradition may be a virgin, or she may be married, though not to the poet; but in either case her chief characteristic is her indomitable chastity. The lover professes his passion and devotion; she treats him with long disdain, and it is her fate to be taken at her word. She is "cruel" and "tyrannous" because she will not yield. . . . But these are passing irritations; the dominant tone is one of ardor and submission. The poet of the traditional sonnet often feels in his heart that his love is wrong, and he sometimes argues against himself on the side of morality—an understandable consequence of his towering idealization of the lady. One feels sometimes that nothing would disconcert him more than the sudden success of his suit. . . . With Shakespeare, however, the essence of love is mutuality. With almost all the others the lover's condition is compared to a wrecked ship; with many the lady's hair is a golden net in which the lover is ensnared. He is desolate and sleepless, and his sighs trouble the heavens. The lady is described in terms of flowers, jewels, and all precious things. Her hair is threads of beaten gold, her forehead crystal, her eyes suns, her cheeks roses, her teeth pearls, her neck ivory or alabaster. Her features are detailed in what has come to be called the descending description. The poet begins with her hair and is restrained only by the limits of his ingenuity and the happy brevity of the sonnet form. . . .

FROM HUMOR TO REGRET TO REMORSE

It turned out that Shakespeare's passion for the dark lady found its only joyous expression in comedy and word-play:

> When my love swears that she is made of truth,
> I do believe her though I know she lies,
> That she might think me some untutor'd youth,
> Unlearned in the world's false subtleties.
> Thus vainly thinking that she thinks me young,
> Although she knows my days are past the best,
> Simply I credit her false speaking tongue:
> On both sides thus is simple truth suppress'd.
> But wherefore says she not she is unjust?
> And wherefore say not I that I am old?
> O, love's best habit is in seeming trust,
> And age in love loves not to have years told:
>   Therefore I lie with her, and she with me,
>   And in our faults by lies we flatter'd be.   (Sonnet 138)

Only a few of the twenty-six poems to the dark lady are in this mood of amused contentment.

Before long there were regrets, a deepening seriousness that made the lover think of his love as lust. . . . The poet's relationship with the dark lady is neither dignified nor prettified; there is not a glimmer of romance. Later the relationship is considered and rejected, but for the time being it simply *is.* . . .

His tenderness does not trap him into sentimentality; his wit never serves as protective coloring, sophisticating the thrust of emotion to an easy obliquity. In the sonnets to the dark lady he accepts the passion, and, later, the remorse. . . .

His portrait as he has drawn it in the sonnets is not flattering. He presents himself as enslaved, and at times he is both witty and vulgar about it.

Away from his lady he imagines her faithless with his friend. Perhaps she is "wooing" the friend's "purity with her foul pride,"

> And whether that my angel be turned fiend,
> Suspect I may, yet not directly tell;
> But being both from me, both to each friend,
> I guess one angel in another's hell. . . .   (Sonnet 144)

Shakespeare's sketch of the dark lady is of a piece with the view of sex without romance revealed throughout his works. He regards it in turn with humor, contentment, rebellion, and revulsion—but never simply or falsely. His view here is no less manifold than his view of life as a whole. The woman is depicted as younger than he—how much younger we cannot know. He seems to have been about thirty when the sonnets were written, and he no doubt felt older. . . .

We may guess that the young woman was in her early twenties. She was married, faithless to her husband in her liaison with the poet, and faithless to them both in her affairs with others. She had "robb'd others' beds' revenues of their rents."[5] And he cannot understand why he thinks her a "several [that is, private] plot" while his heart knows her to be the "wide world's common place."[6] She is the "usurer that put'st forth all to use."[7] In varying moods of reproach he refers to her "unworthiness"[8] and calls her a "cheater,"[9] "covetous,"[10] and "unjust."[11] The ladies of the sonnet tradition were cruel in their chaste denials; the dark lady is cruel because she is gaily promiscuous while enforcing his bondage to her. . . .

THE POWER OF PASSION

The sonnets ask why the heart should be bound by what the eye can see is worthless. The question repeats, and the answer, when it comes, is as familiar as the question: although everyone knows that lust is

> perjur'd, murderous, bloody, full of blame. . . .
>   none knows well
> To shun the heaven that leads men to this hell. (Sonnet 129)

Helpless in the grip of passion, he submits to her, forsaking his better self, trying at times to persuade himself that she is

5. Sonnet 142   6. Sonnet 150   7. Sonnet 138   8. Sonnet 137   9. Sonnet 151   10. Sonnet 134   11. Sonnet 134

better than he knows her to be. He asks her to end the affair by saying that she does not love him, or, in his company, to let it appear that she does. And when it is clear that she will not be true, he begs her in a sonnet of extraordinary plainness to go her way and come back to him later.... The same concept centuries ago created Aphrodite to symbolize the willful and irrational dominance of passion.

In the sonnets Shakespeare writes that his eyes do not find the lady beautiful, that his ears are not delighted with her voice, and that

> Nor taste nor smell desire to be invited
> To any sensual feast with thee alone;
> But my five wits nor my five senses can
> Dissuade one foolish heart from serving thee.... (Sonnet 141)

It is the same simultaneousness of attraction and revulsion which was to become so characteristic of his dramatic treatment of sex in later years.... The unhappiness is presented in itself as a commonly observed aspect of life. The passion which dominates and tortures is thought of as a manifestation of man's natural self. The view of human nature is not optimistic; there are *at once* incalculable potentials for both good and evil....

Shakespeare's works assume the reality of both good and evil, and while it is once or twice suggested that a certain trait of character is the result of training (the only notable instance is Coriolanus)[12] sexual evil is never presented as the manifestation of a neurosis.... The poet of the sonnets comes to think of his love as a thing without health, as a fever always longing "for that which longer nurseth the disease." He comes to loathe his passion, and his loathing swells until it includes both himself and the dark lady:

> For I have sworn thee fair and thought thee bright,
> Who art as black as hell, as dark as night.   (Sonnet 147)

TRIUMPH OVER PASSION

The sonnets of deepest revulsion present an agony which cannot contain itself.... With Shakespeare it moved to a magnification of the spirit and a renunciation of the flesh, set forth in a sonnet of admirable compactness and, once the precision of its grammatical references are noticed, of perfect clarity:

---

12. in *The Tragedy of Coriolanus*

Poor soul, the center[13] of my sinful earth,
Thrall to[14] these rebel powers that thee array,
Why dost thou pine within and suffer dearth,
Painting thy outward walls so costly gay?
Why so large cost, having so short a lease,
Dost thou upon thy fading mansion spend?
Shall worms, inheritors of this excess,
Eat up thy charge?[15] is this thy body's end?
Then soul, live thou upon thy servant's[16] loss,
And let that pine to aggravate[17] thy store;
Buy terms divine[18] in selling hours of dross,[19]
Within be fed, without be rich no more:
  So shalt thou feed on death, that feeds on men,
  And death once dead, there's no more dying then.

(Sonnet 146)

There is nothing with which the sonnets are more insistently concerned than with the aspiration to triumph over death. In the early sonnets immortality is to be won through propagation and poetry. At the close it is to be found in the salvation of the soul. Throughout there is a progressive growth in moral emphasis. I do not suggest, of course, that the sonnets are primarily a sequence of moral poems; and it should be pointed out that although the recognition of lust extends over many poems, there is only one poem which renounces the flesh. Still, the poem exists and seems to be the culmination of the sonnets to the dark lady. . . .

The triumph here is that of the spirit over sin, and in the light of this triumph death takes on insignificance. No one supposes that all readers of Shakespeare will share this belief, but it is a little late to deny the use of it to Shakespeare. The exhortation to his soul to find eternal life in shattering his sexual enslavement is an understandable consequence of the passion he describes.

13. Elizabethans saw the earth as the center of the universe.   14. "Thrall to," or slave to, is a widely accepted conjectural emendation. In the original text the line begins with a manifest error.   15. what you have spent   16. body's   17. increase   18. immortal life   19. worthlessness

Shakespeare's Sonnets Explore the Meaning of Time

David Kaula

David Kaula argues that Shakespeare's sonnets addressing a friend, Nos. 1–126, are a study of time and its importance. According to Kaula, Shakespeare's view of time changes within these sonnets. In the early poems, Shakespeare presents time as a cosmic power that will destroy his friend since its power destroys all things eventually. Only two possibilities can stop time's destruction: His friend can marry and father a son who will inherit his beauty, or the sonnets themselves will live into the future and immortalize the friend. Kaula then analyzes Sonnet 60, in which the poet's friend will live on in the poem. In the later sonnets, Shakespeare presents time simply as a record of the personal changes in a continuing friendship. Over time, a relationship of love can grow stronger by overcoming adversity. Kaula calls the first view objective and the second subjective.

David Kaula, a professor of English at Dartmouth College, has contributed articles to scholarly journals.

The figure of time which occurs so often in the sonnets Shakespeare addresses to the young friend (1–126) points to one of the central preoccupations of the sequence. Appearing as it does in several of its familiar allegorical guises—as thief, tyrant, devourer, and harvester—the figure is thoroughly conventional in origin. Shakespeare, however, endows it with a more than conventional[1] vitality. . . . By making versatile use of varying time perspectives, both objective and subjective, Shakespeare further deepens and diversifies

1. from conventions, the standard practices of poets

Excerpted from "In War with Time: Temporal Perspectives in Shakespeare's Sonnets" by David Kaula, *Studies in English Literature, 1500–1900*, vol. 3, no. 1, Winter 1963. Reprinted by permission of *Studies in English Literature, 1500–1900*.

his handling of the poet-friend relationship, and partly because of this he manages to avoid that monotonous rehearsal of stock attitudes which cripples all but a few of the Elizabethan sonnet sequences.

In view of the conceptions of time they embody, the sonnets to the friend may be divided into two fairly distinct groups. In the first, made up largely of the sonnets urging the friend to procreate and those that promise to immortalize him in the poet's verse, time is conceived in large mythic dimensions. It is a cosmic power which operates on all levels of creation and keeps them in constant flux, relentlessly destroying everything it produces. Its workings are conveyed chiefly through images of recurrent natural processes: the round of the seasons, day and night, the sun in its rise and decline, organic growth and decay, the interchange of sea and land. Equally expansive are the references to past and future, extending as far backward as the "holy antique hours" of the Golden Age (67, 68), and as far ahead as the "judgment" (55) or "edge of doom" (116). In these sonnets the poet maintains a fixed attitude towards the friend, that of formal, somewhat distant admiration, together with a concern for what in the long-range view the friend must suffer along with the rest of creation under the tyranny of time.

But in the other group, the relationship, rather than being accepted as an unchanging fact, is explored and responded to as a developing situation. It assumes, in other words, a history, having a definite beginning ("when first your eye I ey'd" [104]), proceeding through various phases of estrangement and reconciliation, and having a potential ending in either the poet's death or the friend's disaffection. Hence the time perspectives in these sonnets are more restricted in scope, more subjective in orientation than those in the first group. The harmful varieties of time, those which work against the relationship, are associated not with natural processes but with social activities of the modish or opportunistic kind, such as commerce, the law, social and literary fads, and status-seeking at court. To these the poet opposes a form of time whose main characteristic is unassailable constancy, though it also includes a distinctive pattern of growth and renewal. . . .

An image of particular significance in the procreation group—it is developed most fully in Sonnet 7—is that of the sun. Like the latter the friend's life follows a curving pattern, steadily rising until it reaches its "highmost pitch," all the while receiving the homage of mankind. Repeatedly the friend is told, in combination of warning and compliment, that he presently stands at the zenith of the curve: "Thou that art now the world's fresh ornament" (1); "this thy golden time" (3); "Now stand you at the top of happy hours" (16). But from the foreshortened view of time implicit in the sun analogy, this present perfection appears alarmingly brief and vulnerable, since it is at this point that wasteful Time begins its debate with Decay (15), and the only direction the sun-friend can travel is downward into night.

TWO STRATEGIES TO OVERCOME THE DESTRUCTION BROUGHT ON BY TIME

To compensate for the inevitable descent the poet proposes two strategies. One, the friend's presenting the world with a copy of himself in the form of offspring, would have the effect of converting the single, finite curve into a cycle. Like the sun he can rise again—as one of Shakespeare's less felicitous puns has it—by producing a son (7). The other strategy, the preservation of the friend's "living" memory in deathless verse, would convert the curve at its apex into a straight line extending into the remote future, the friend's temporary summer thereby becoming an "eternal" one (18). Although both strategies are metaphorical translations[2] of the same desire, poetically the second is more persuasive than the first. . . .

Since the perpetuation will be limited to one repetition of the cycle, extending no further into the future than the "age to come" (17), time in the long-range view will ultimately win out. Yet another difficulty, reflected in the rhetorical qualities of the procreation sonnets, is that the poet is obliged to play a passive, hortatory[3] role, subservient to the will of what appears to be a recalcitrant, narcissistic Mr. W.H. (or whoever the friend might be). The poet can only argue and beseech; the friend himself must choose to take the step which will counteract the onslaught of time. After a tentative comparison of the two strategies in Sonnets 16 and 17, the poet displays a greater confidence when he finally settles on his own verse as a means of perpetuation in 18 and 19. For now it is he who is actively putting the strategy into effect, its

2. from metaphor, a figure of speech in which a comparison is implied, not stated
3. urging

success depending not on the friend's cooperativeness but on the strength of his own devotion distilled in his immortal lines. Accordingly he expands his vision of the present's continuation into the future from the relatively limited "age to come" to the far-reaching "eternal summer.". . .

GREATER CONFIDENCE THAT TIME CAN BE OVERCOME

After the repeated qualifications of the procreation group, Sonnet 18, with its confident use of the emphatic future tense in the third quatrain ("But thy eternal summer shall not fade"), introduces a markedly new tone into the sequence. It appears again in Sonnet 19, where the poet for the first time directly addresses "Devouring Time" in the second person, concluding his apostrophe[4] with the vigorous challenge of the couplet:

> Yet do thy worst, old Time: despite thy wrong,
> My love shall in my verse ever live young.

. . . The technique[5] becomes the more evident when Shakespeare's handling is compared with one of the principal sources of his imagery. In Pythagoras's discourse in Book XV of the *Metamorphoses*, Ovid describes the mutability of all things as a slow, repetitive flux, like the flowing of a river or the movement of waves. Time for him works by gradual attrition: it nibbles its victims rather than bolts them down:

> O Time, thou great devourer, and thou, envious Age, together
> you destroy all things; and, slowly gnawing with your teeth,
> you finally consume all things in lingering death.

In keeping with this conception of time, Ovid presents the course of human life as a gradual rise and fall proceeding through several intermediate stages. . . .

In Sonnet 60 ("Like as the waves make towards the pebbled shore")—one of those which most clearly shows the Ovidian influence—Shakespeare first describes the ceaseless, wave-like procession of minutes; then, in the second quatrain, sharply compresses the Ovidian life-cycle:

> Nativity, once in the main of light,
> Crawls to maturity, wherewith being crown'd,
> Crooked eclipses 'gainst his glory fight,
> And Time that gave doth now his gift confound.

The rising movement of the first two lines, prolonged by the

4. direct address of an absent or imaginary person or thing   5. of magnifying time's importance by foreshortening or accelerating it

caesuras, is abruptly arrested at its climax by the "Crooked eclipses," and the subsequent decline is swift and final, the process being succinctly recapitulated in the fourth line in the double action of time's giving and confounding. Now that he has explicitly identified the prime antagonist, Shakespeare proceeds in the third quatrain to delineate time's frontal assault on man and nature through a series of aggressive present-tense verbs:

> Time doth transfix the flourish set on youth
> And delves the parallels in beauty's brow,
> Feeds on the rarities of nature's truth,
> And nothing stands but for his scythe to mow.

As ruthless as he makes time appear, Shakespeare does not regard it with the melancholy resignation of Ovid. Instead, the power he ascribes to it becomes, in a manner analogous to the primitive rhetorical technique of controlling-by-naming, his own: the more formidable the opponent, the more firmly dedicated he is to its victims, the more determined he is to resist its tyranny. Thus he concludes the sonnet with the characteristic defiance stated in the emphatic future:

> And yet to times in hope my verse shall stand,
> Praising thy worth, despite his cruel hand.

TIME MEASURES THE CHANGING RELATIONSHIP WITH HIS FRIEND

... The sonnets in the other group, those which exploit the varieties of subjective time, presuppose a different relationship between poet and friend. The friend here is not, or should not be, the cynosure[6] of an adoring world; nor is the poet the self-effacing spokesman for that world. They in their private relationship stand apart from the public realm. ...

A recurrent danger to the relationship is that the friend, in being "woo'd of time" (70) or the fashions of the age, will permit himself to be absorbed by the public world, adopting its changeableness, and thus jeopardize those singular qualities which make him so remarkable in the poet's eyes. The first indication in the sequence that something like this has happened, that there has been a development in the relationship beyond the static situation assumed in the other group of sonnets, occurs in Sonnet 33 ("Full many a glorious morning have I seen"). Whatever the "region cloud" that

6. a focal point or guide

comes between him and his "sun" may signify, the poet emphasizes the fact of present alienation by speaking of the friend in the third person rather than addressing him, as he usually does, in the second, and by using the past and present perfect tenses:

> But out alack! he was but one hour mine,
> The region cloud hath mask'd him from me now.

. . . In Sonnet 30 ("When to the sessions of sweet silent thought"), for instance, the movement from frustration to release coincides with the transference of awareness from past to present, from the memory of irretrievable losses to the recognition that they are now fully redeemed through the compensation provided by the friend. Here Shakespeare presents the saddening finitude of things not as a condition of the universe at large, objectified in the figure of time, but as something perceived and suffered inwardly. . . .

In the later sonnets of the series, those which indicate in various ways that the friendship has lasted a considerable time,[7] we see repeated evidence of Shakespeare's awareness that his devotion is anything but a static ideal religiously adhered to, that it is a lived experience which changes and develops in time. This implies a new, positive conception of time, one which is closely involved with the poet's surer sense of his role both towards the friend and towards the world at large. Having weathered past uncertainties and humiliations, betrayals both feared and actual, he can now claim: "My love is strengthened, though more weak in seeming" (102); or, "Now with the drops of this most balmy time My love looks fresh" (107); or, in lines which anticipate the progression from alienation to atonement in the late comedies:

> O benefit of ill! Now I find true
> That better is by evil still made better,
> And ruin'd love, when it is built anew,
> Grows fairer than at first, more strong, far greater.   (119)

From this new vantage point the poet is able to place both past and future in truer perspective. He sees that his earlier anxiety over the possibility of change, his "fearing of Time's tyranny" (115), had provoked him into exalting the present moment as final and supreme, into proclaiming "Now I love you best"; whereas subsequent experience has shown that the future, rather than being considered a threat, can be ac-

---

7. three years, according to Sonnet 104

cepted as an opportunity for further growth. Similarly, he sees the old enemy, cosmic time, in a different light. Instead of lamenting the impermanence of earthly things, he regards time with an equanimity that verges on satirical contempt, even when he observes its effects on the friend:

> Rise, resty Muse, my love's sweet face survey,
> If Time have any wrinkle graven there;
> If any, be a satire to decay,
> And make Time's spoils despised everywhere.   (100)

Thus the figure of time is no longer the predatory colossus it was in the first group of sonnets. It is now sly and insidious in its action, deceiving humanity through the "million'd accidents.". . .

A POSITIVE VIEW OF TIME CENTERED IN PERSONAL EXPERIENCE

The strategy[8] is to reduce the negative form of time and the domain it governs to trivial proportions, and to replace it with another, positive conception of time which is squarely centered in the poet's personal experience and intimately associated with his achieved sense of stability. Confidently oriented in the present, without regret for the past or anxiety for the future, the poet in the end is able to make unapologetic use of the first person pronoun in asserting "I am that I am" (121); and of his love for the friend he is able to claim, finally, that it "all alone stands hugely politic" (124), sufficient to itself, unintimidated by the public world and its exaggerated interest in transitory things.

The two groups of sonnets in general show Shakespeare's imagination working in contrasting ways. In the one, he draws upon the allegorical tradition as it is represented, say, in the iconographic images[9] of Father Time and in Spenser's Mutabilitie.[10] He conceives time mainly in pictorial terms as a figure of cosmic dimensions. . . . Exploring the qualities of time as it is directly experienced, he illuminates the varying perspectives in which past, present and future appear in response to his developing awareness of himself and his relationship to the friend. It is primarily in his handling of time in these latter sonnets that Shakespeare points ahead to his mature dramatic practise.

---

8. for combating time   9. from *icon*, an image, representation, or symbol   10. change that brings the end of life, from "The Mutability Cantos" by Edmund Spenser

Shakespeare Searches for Immortality in the Sonnets

George Herbert Palmer

In presenting the 1912 Ingersoll Lecture on the Immortality of Man, George Herbert Palmer uses Shakespeare's sonnets to illustrate his views on immortality. He declares that immortality is unachievable, but spiritual immortality can at least be glimpsed in private. He says that Shakespeare did not make the young man in his sonnets immortal. But when Shakespeare despairs of his evil experiences with the dark woman in Sonnet 146, he experiences a moment of spiritual immortality, when he feels "there is no more dying" for his "Poor soul." To clarify this experience, Palmer names and defines four kinds of immortality. Ideal immortality, the notion that a human can live forever, is self-deception used to soften harsh reality. Individual immortality is a private experience within the conscious mind. Spiritual immortality occurs when an individual knows himself or herself as a moral person who can take charge of personal events. Natural immortality occurs when a person lives on in children born in future generations.

George Herbert Palmer was a professor of philosophy at Harvard from 1873 to 1913. He is well known for his scholarly works on Greek and English literature.

Ideal Immortality is something which the desolate hearts of every age have tried to comfort themselves with. In this course it has been advocated as equivalent to immortality itself. And poetic though it is, it forms indeed a good sort of secondary solace, preventing the world from seeming altogether hostile, and introducing into familiar places, now

Excerpted from *Intimations of Immortality in the Sonnets of Shakespeare* by George Herbert Palmer (Boston: Houghton Mifflin, 1912).

painfully vacant, a kind of communion with him who is not there. But he is not there; let us acknowledge it. No profit comes of self-deception. Ideal Immortality expresses no fact, however pleasant a fancy it is to play with.

That fact, the reality of Individual Immortality, is not indeed a matter open to external observation. It cannot be detected in the case of another person, but must be come at in the consciousness of the man himself. The complete conception of immortality—at least, Spiritual Immortality, in which we know ourselves as moral beings, capable of commanding time and circumstance instead of accepting their compulsions—is something which cannot be imparted, but must be reached in a person's own experience. The third group of Sonnets to which we now turn records such an experience of Shakspere's.

THE DARK WOMAN: A BAD EXPERIENCE

It shows him at a time of bitter temptation—yes, of monstrous and degrading sin; for even while dedicated to lofty things by love of the beautiful youth, he yields to the allurements of a woman whom he despises. She possesses little physical attraction other than her bewitching eyes, has coarse dark hair and a dark complexion, both regarded as blemishes in Elizabeth's time, strikingly red lips, a voice not altogether pleasing, is older than Shakspere, and known by him to be an adulteress already. Yet he is fascinated, fascinated even while repelled. He cannot escape from her dark eyes, imperious ways, and feminine caprices. He tells us that while "her face hath not the power to make love groan," "her will is large and spacious," and she "hath the strength and warrantise of skill." She is of musical temperament and incomprehensibly dominates him, arraying him against himself as Cleopatra does Marc Antony.[1] It is a squalid story.

With one side of his nature he knows that all that is of worth in him is destroyed by contact with her; with another he feels there is no life for him except in her presence. But she is not content with his single abasement.[2] She seeks the friend too, and, as Shakspere believes, with success:—

Two loves I have of comfort and despair,
Which like two spirits do suggest[3] me still:
The better angel is a man right fair,

1. in Shakespeare's play *The Tragedy of Antony and Cleopatra*   2. act of lowering or submission   3. tempt

The worser spirit a woman colour'd ill.
To win me soon to hell, my female evil
Tempteth my better angel from my side,
And would corrupt my saint to be a devil,
Wooing his purity with her foul pride.
And whether that my angel be turn'd fiend
Suspect I may, yet not directly tell;
But being both from me, both to each friend,[4]
I guess one angel in another's hell;
    Yet this shall I ne'er know, but live in doubt,
    Till my bad angel fire my good one out.   (Sonnet 144)

This alienation of the friend through the machinations[5] of
the dark lady is already touched on in the preceding series
of sonnets, especially in those from thirty-three to forty-two
and from ninety-two to ninety-six. But wherever it is mentioned little blame is attached to the youth. Shakspere's hor-
ror is directed almost entirely against himself, that he could
be base enough to be enslaved by one so worthless. He is as-
tonished and afflicted. Yet it is the very sense of this inner
tragedy as constituting the essence of sin which gradually
brings him to an understanding of Spiritual Immortality.
The story of his misery and of his ultimate hope of relief
forms the subject of the final series of sonnets, though here
it is not probable that the separate pieces have been printed
in their original order.

    At the beginning, when Shakspere first sees the dark lady
seated at her spinnet, there is no thought of misery. All is
gladness and the sense of incoming life:—

How oft, when thou, my music, music play'st,
Upon that blessèd wood[6] whose motion sounds
With thy sweet fingers, when thou gently sway'st
The wiry concord[7] that mine ear confounds
Do I envy those jacks[8] that nimble leap
To kiss the tender inward of thy hand,
Whilst my poor lips, which should that harvest reap,
At the wood's boldness by thee blushing stand!
To be so tickled, they would change their state
And situation with those dancing chips,
O'er whom thy fingers walk with gentle gait,
Making dead wood more bless'd than living lips.
    Since saucy jacks so happy are in this,
    Give them thy fingers, me thy lips to kiss.   (Sonnet 128)

    But as the affair proceeds, an inner conflict is disclosed
and inward bitterness:—

---

4. friends to each other 5. destructive schemes 6. the keys of the virginal, a small,
legless harpsichord 7. harmony of wires 8. keys of the virginal

My love is as a fever, longing still
For that which longer nurseth the disease;
Feeding on that which doth preserve the ill,
Th' uncertain sickly appetite to please.
My reason, the physician to my love,
Angry that his prescriptions are not kept,
Hath left me, and I desperate now approve[9]
Desire is death, which physic did except.[10]
Past cure I am, now reason is past care,
And frantic-mad with evermore unrest;
My thoughts and my discourse as madmen's are,
At random from the truth vainly express'd;
　For I have sworn thee fair and thought thee bright,
　Who art as black as hell, as dark as night.　　(Sonnet 147)

The expense of spirit in a waste of shame
Is lust in action; and till action, lust
Is perjured, murderous, bloody, full of blame,
Savage, extreme, rude, cruel, not to trust;
Enjoy'd no sooner but despisèd straight;
Past reason hunted; and no sooner had,
Past reason hated, as a swallowed bait,
On purpose laid to make the taker mad;
Mad in pursuit, and in possession so;
Had, having, and in quest to have, extreme;
A bliss in proof; and proved,[11] a very woe;
Before, a joy proposed; behind, a dream.
　All this the world well knows; yet none knows well
　To shun the heaven that leads men to this hell.
　　　　　　　　　　　　　　　　　　(Sonnet 129)

THE POET'S LOW POINT

In this last sonnet is the lowest depth to which Shakspere describes himself as sinking. And precisely here, in the intensity and bewilderment of sin, the possibility of a Spiritual Immortality is revealed. Within himself he discovers an immortal nature at issue with the forces of mortality. A true self is set in contrast with the changing, conflicting, enslaving passions. Of these "rebel powers," the expression only of time and sense, he can now say with the Apostle: "They are not I, but sin that dwelleth in me."

In the one hundred and forty-sixth Sonnet, which might well stand as the conclusion of the entire series, he speaks out with extraordinary fervor and precision his hope of victory over these "hours of dross":—

---

9. prove by experience　10. forbid　11. experienced

Poor soul, the centre[12] of my sinful earth,
Fool'd by these rebel powers that thee array,
Why dost thou pine within and suffer dearth,
Painting thy outward walls so costly gay?
Why so large cost, having so short a lease,
Dost thou upon thy fading mansion spend?
Shall worms, inheritors of this excess,
Eat up thy charge?[13] Is this thy body's end?
Then, soul, live thou upon thy servant's[14] loss,
And let that pine, to aggravate[15] thy store;
Buy terms divine[16] in selling hours of dross;
Within be fed, without be rich no more.
   So shalt thou feed on Death, that feeds on men,
   And, Death once dead, there's no more dying then.

(Sonnet 146)

Here is Spiritual Immortality. Man is a spirit, no mere creature of circumstance, passive, instantaneous, dependent on alien forces within and without, which sweep him along their blind current, regardless of any good of his own. He is an active being, dictatorial over time and circumstance, with power to compel chance and change to work for his permanent welfare. Such an understanding of immortality, grounded in the nature of personality, gives a hope more specific than the Ideal Immortality of fame, more humanly significant than the Natural Immortality of "breed."

But as I thus formulate Shakspere's contribution to our knowledge of the momentous problem which this lectureship was founded to discuss, I suspect my hearers must often have questioned whether I am drawing my threefold doctrine from the Sonnets themselves or am reading it into them. Did Shakspere plan anything of that sort? Did he mean to announce a theological doctrine with three stages of successively larger hope? No; he certainly never meant that, but nevertheless it meant him. And just because he had not intended to be a philosophic teacher, but gave his mind whole-heartedly to the lovely boy and his own temptation, I have thought him a suitable person to invite to this platform.

IMMORTALITY GROUNDED IN CONCRETE EXPERIENCE

We treat immortality too much as an affair of abstract speculation. But if it possesses any worth, it must be discoverable among the concrete experiences of life and there be a covert force operating on us at all times. Perhaps we can best un-

12. Elizabethans believed the earth was the center of the universe.   13. what you have spent   14. body's   15. increase   16. immortal life

derstand it by approaching somebody who does not understand it and studying how it gets its hold on him. For this purpose I summon Shakspere. Few writers of our language, I suppose, are so little theological as he; few so little disposed to report their own beliefs. He is therefore an unbiased and typical witness to the necessity and meaning of immortality.

In the exigencies[17] of the day he has come upon it. Mortality has proved unthinkable. He has been unable to state his deepest experiences except in terms of permanence. Whether the story related is fact or fiction makes no difference. Its likeness to reality is gained—as in human intercourse generally—only through treating its characters as immortal beings. That I have given his underlying assumptions undue prominence, I fully admit. Shakspere's attention was not fixed on them, as I desire yours to be. It was busy with a multi-colored life in which single events stood out more strongly than embodied principles. I have accordingly announced in my title that these guiding thoughts appear only as "intimations."[18] Yet it cannot be too insistently asserted that they form the very framework of the Sonnets, and that English criticism has too long passed them by while busying itself about the identity of "Mr. W.H."

Whoever he was, the poems get their universal human worth from the fact that Shakspere, brooding over the love of his friend, encounters perplexities of time and eternity. . . . These anxious and sorrowing lovers, shocked by the onslaughts of time, grope after a vision of immortality and undogmatically disclose to us what each severally finds.

SHAKSPERE FAILS TO MAKE THE YOUNG MAN IMMORTAL

Some of my hearers may be disposed to ask whether "that eternitie promised by our ever-living poet" was actually secured. Taking up the forms of immortality here intimated, can we call Shakspere successful in ultimately attaining any of the three? Hardly, I think; at least the scanty evidence is chiefly of a negative kind. For first, the young man is to marry and be perpetuated through a long line of descendants. Later ages will understand his beauty through his offspring. Was it so? Apparently not. We do not learn whether he married and had children. But if he did, "breed" did not save him. His son has been lost in the undistinguished mass

17. the urgency of personal crises   18. hints or suggestions

of mankind and bears no marks of his father.

But ideas are trustier than nature, and surely Shakspere has been successful in giving the beautiful boy Ideal Immortality? Not at all. We do not know who he was. His name perished before it was ever uttered, and has been for three centuries a subject of eager dispute. Perhaps it was Pembroke, perhaps Southampton, perhaps one of a multitude of less famous claimants. We are not likely ever to learn. Yet Shakspere may have wished to hide the name the better to perpetuate the character, and in these Sonnets the portrait stands as magical and lasting as Leonardo's Mona Lisa. Magical indeed it is, but indistinct in every feature.

Of his appearance, interests, characteristics, or circumstances, almost nothing is told. That he was beautiful and loved is substantially all. His hair was like marjoram buds, whatever color that may be. There are hints of wealth and high station. If he was pleased to have Shakspere address him these subtle verses, he had intellectual tastes. But how shadowy a figure! No personal traits, no glimpses of feature, no casual incidents have come down to us. Even the type of his beauty is unreported. It is strange. Repeatedly Shakspere declares his purpose of immortalizing his friend; but fails to do so, takes indeed no steps to accomplish it, and merely immortalizes the friendship. The portrait given shows only such generalized outlines as those of Shelley's Keats and has none of the specific individuality which Tennyson gave Hallam. The praise of the boy therefore survives, his praiser will never die, but the boy himself is gone.

And then the third, the culminating ideal. Shakspere saw his passions to be matters of a moment, and so by contrast became aware of an imperial Self which could not be subjected to temporary influences without shame.

> He felt through all his earthly dress
> Bright shoots of everlastingness.[19]

Was he true to that deep insight? Through its light was he able to picture so clearly the long line of diversified human beings with which he has enriched the world? Or did he lose himself again in solicitations[20] of the flesh? Who but himself can say? Once at least, we know, he looked into immortality.

---

19. from "The Retreat" by seventeenth-century Welsh poet Henry Vaughan   20. temptations or enticements

CHAPTER 4

Analysis of Individual Sonnets

READINGS ON
THE SONNETS

Prose Versions of Seven Sonnets

A.L. Rowse

A.L. Rowse says he is certain that Shakespeare's sonnet series is autobiographical and that it tells a "dramatic" story. With that assumption in mind, Rowse has transposed each sonnet into prose to make the story more intelligible to modern readers. His "practical and common sense" method, Rowse says, finally gives readers the meaning of Shakespeare's text. Even though Rowse recommends reading the entire sonnet series from beginning to end, as one would a play or novel, only a few of the best known sonnets have been selected to represent Rowse's argument.

A leading expert on Elizabethan England, A.L. Rowse has taught at All Souls College, Oxford; and the Huntington Library, San Marino, California. A member of the Royal Society of Literature in England, he has published an extensive list of books, one of which, a biography of Shakespeare, shocked critics because he claims to have identified conclusively the woman in the sonnets.

Hitherto the Sonnets of Shakespeare have been regarded as the greatest puzzle in English, possibly world, literature. Their problems have been thought to be insoluble, the questions they raise unanswerable. In default of answers, certain and valid, these poems—among the world's most famous and beautiful—have long provided ground for the wildest speculation. Even among scholars there has been no certainty, but utter confusion. Their very nature has been in dispute, some respectable scholars thinking them to have been mere literary exercises.

They were, of course, autobiographical; they would not have the power, the urgency and conviction they carry, if

Excerpted from *Shakespeare's Sonnets: The Problems Solved* by A.L. Rowse, 2nd ed. (New York: Harper & Row, 1973). Copyright ©1964, 1973 by A.L. Rowse. Reprinted by permission of Curtis Brown Ltd.

they had not been. They were autobiography before they became literature. They come straight from the heart, from the whole personality—as great literature does—of the world's best loved writer. Naturally, with a professional writer, they have here and there touches of literary exercise; but, as a whole, they tell a story so strange that it could only have been experienced and true.

It is the purpose of this edition to bring out the story, as none has been able to do, and to show that it *is* true. One cannot fully appreciate the Sonnets without reading them as a whole: no use reaching one down here or there and then hoping to grasp the situation and what one is being told. Yet that is what people usually do.

A HISTORIAN'S APPROACH TO THE SONNETS

The Sonnets were never written to create a puzzle—though the clue has been lost for centuries. They were written straightforwardly, directly, by one person for another—by a poet for his young patron, as we shall see—with an immediate and sincere impulse. Yet the story that is revealed, and has been concealed for so long, is highly dramatic and that of a poet who was already beginning to be well known as a dramatist. That is why they were not published at the time, like other sonnet-sequences; they were not published till years after the story they relate was folded up, and then not by Shakespeare, but by a publisher who had *got* the manuscripts. . . .

As I have said all along, the proper method is an historical one: to take each poem one after the other, to follow it line by line, watching for every piece of internal information for its coherence with what is happening in the external world, checking for consistency at every point, accumulating patiently every fact and what may legitimately be inferred, until the whole structure stands forth clear. I said originally that it would be found that the historian's account of the matter could not be impugned. . . .

Actually my text is closer to the original and more conservative than any other. The historian who has been habituated to Elizabethan usage all his life and has read thousands of original documents, finds their language becomes second nature to him. This has useful literary consequences. Many people misjudge the relations between the poet and his patron by thinking of the high-flown language in modern terms: they are not sufficiently deep in the age to know that this was the proper decorum for a gentlemanly poet to use to a handsome young nobleman. Even textually, an Elizabethan scholar realises that there is no need for the emendations and interferences with the text that Georgian and Victorian editors felt called upon to make. They are just not necessary. . . .

The object of the version in modern prose is again *intelligibility*, to bring out the meaning. Here, too, I have been conservative rather than adventurous: I have kept closely to Shakespeare's own words, so far as the differing rhythms of prose and verse allow. . . .

SONNET 18

Shall I compare thee to a summer's day?
Thou art more lovely and more temperate:
Rough winds do shake the darling buds of May,
And summer's lease hath all too short a date:
Sometime too hot the eye of heaven shines,
And often is his gold complexion dimmed;
And every fair from fair sometime declines,
By chance or nature's changing course untrimmed.
But thy eternal summer shall not fade,
Nor lose possession of that fair thou ow'st;
Nor shall death brag thou wander'st in his shade,
When in eternal lines to time thou grow'st:
   So long as men can breathe, or eyes can see,
   So long lives this, and this gives life to thee.

Shall I compare you to a summer's day? You are more gracious and even tempered. Rough winds shake the buds of May, and summer is all too short: sometimes the sun is too hot, or often is clouded over; everything that is fair loses its beauty, by chance or in the course of nature coarsened. But your eternal summer shall not fade, nor lose the beauty that belongs to it; nor shall death boast possession of you, when in eternal verse you grow one with time. So long as men can breathe, or eyes can see, so long will this live, giving you immortality. . . .

SONNET 29

When, in disgrace with fortune and men's eyes,
I all alone beweep my outcast state,
And trouble deaf heaven with my bootless cries,
And look upon myself, and curse my fate:
Wishing me like to one more rich in hope,
Featured like him, like him with friends possessed,

Desiring this man's art and that man's scope,
With what I most enjoy contented least:
Yet in these thoughts myself almost despising,
Haply I think on thee, and then my state,
Like to the lark at break of day arising
From sullen earth, sings hymns at heaven's gate;
   For thy sweet love remembered such wealth brings
   That then I scorn to change my state with kings.

When down on my luck and with people set against me, all alone I lament my lot as an outsider: but I reproach heaven in vain with my laments, looking upon myself and cursing my fate. I wish myself like one with more hope in life, like him in looks and surrounded with friends; I find myself envying this man's art and that man's range, least contented with what I most enjoy. In this mood almost despising myself, I happen to think of you: and then, like the lark rising at dawn from sullen earth, I chant hymns to heaven. For thinking of your love brings such wealth to mind that then I would not change my state with kings....

SONNET 30

When to the sessions of sweet silent thought
I summon up remembrance of things past,
I sigh the lack of many a thing I sought
And with old woes new wail my dear time's waste:
Then can I drown an eye, unused to flow,
For precious friends hid in death's dateless night,
And weep afresh love's long since cancelled woe,
And moan the expense of many a vanished sight:
Then can I grieve at grievances foregone,
And heavily from woe to woe tell o'er
The sad account of fore-bemoanèd moan,
Which I new pay as if not paid before.
   But if the while I think on thee, dear friend,
   All losses are restored and sorrows end.

When in these sessions of silent thought I recall memories of past things, I lament the lack of many a thing I wished for and turn over old sorrows with new regrets: then can I weep, though not much given to tears, for beloved friends now dead; bewail anew the wounds of former love, regretting what many a vanished sight has cost me. Then can I grieve at past troubles again, and tell over the account of sorrows already lamented, as if I had not paid the score long ago. But if in this mood I think of you, dear friend, all losses are restored and sorrows over....

SONNET 65

Since brass, nor stone, nor earth, nor boundless sea,
But sad mortality o'er-sways their power,
How with this rage shall beauty hold a plea
Whose action is no stronger than a flower?
O, how shall summer's honey breath hold out
Against the wreckful siege of battering days,
When rocks impregnable are not so stout,
Nor gates of steel so strong, but Time decays?
O fearful meditation! where, alack,
Shall Time's best jewel from Time's chest lie hid?
Or what strong hand can hold his swift foot back?
Or who his spoil of beauty can forbid?
   O, none, unless this miracle have might,
   That in black ink my love may still shine bright.

Since brass and stone, earth and sea, are subject to mortality, how can beauty withstand that force, when its strength is no greater than a flower's? Or how shall the honey-eyed breath of summer hold out against the battering storm of time, when rocks and gates of iron are not so strong but time decays them. A fearful thought! for where, alas, shall Time's best jewel be hid from Time's dark chest? Or what strong hand can stay his foot? Or who can arrest his ravages upon beauty? None, unless there is hope in this miracle, that my love may ever shine bright out of this black ink. . . .

SONNET 73

That time of year thou mayst in me behold
When yellow leaves, or none, or few, do hang
Upon those boughs which shake against the cold,
Bare, ruined choirs,[1] where late the sweet birds sang.
In me thou see'st the twilight of such day
As after sunset fadeth in the west,
Which by and by black night doth take away,
Death's second self, that seals up all in rest.
In me thou see'st the glowing of such fire
That on the ashes of his youth doth lie
As the death-bed whereon it must expire,
Consumed with that which it was nourished by.
   This thou perceiv'st, which makes thy love more strong
   To love that well which thou must leave ere long.

In me you behold that time of year when a few yellow

---

1. 'Bare, ruined choirs' brings to the eye the roofless shells of monastic churches which stood out rawly to anyone travelling round England in the latter part of the sixteenth century; and 'where late the sweet birds sang' carries a characteristic double suggestion of the vanished singing. This seems to be a winter sonnet, the winter of 1592–3.

leaves or none at all hang on the branches, shaking in the
cold, like bare, ruined choirs, where lately birds were
singing. In me you see such twilight as there is after the sun
has faded in the west, which by and by is extinguished by
night—image of death, that seals up all. In me you see the
glow of embers, the ashes of my youth, dying out as on a
death-bed, consumed by that which fed it and gave it life.
Seeing this increases your love and makes you value more
that which you must take leave of before long. . . .

SONNET 116

Let me not to the marriage of true minds
Admit impediments: love is not love
Which alters when it alteration finds,
Or bends with the remover to remove.
O, no! it is an ever-fixéd mark
That looks on tempests and is never shaken;
It is the star to every wandering bark,
Whose worth's unknown, although his height be taken.
Love's not Time's fool, though rosy lips and cheeks
Within his bending sickle's compass come;
Love alters not with his brief hours and weeks,
But bears it out even to the edge of doom:
   If this be error and upon me proved,
   I never writ, nor no man ever loved.

Let me not admit impediments to the marriage of true
minds: love is not love which alters when it meets with alteration, or changes when one of them changes. No, it is a
fixed beacon that looks on storms and is not shaken; it is the
star to every voyaging ship, whose value is not calculable although its altitude is. Love is not the sport of Time, though
rosy lips and cheeks come within the compass of his sickle;
love does not alter with the days, but keeps straight on to the
threshold of doomsday. If this be error proved against me, I
never wrote and no man ever loved. . . .

SONNET 130

My mistress' eyes are nothing like the sun,
Coral is far more red than her lips' red;
If snow be white, why then her breasts are dun,
If hairs be wires, black wires grow on her head.
I have seen roses damasked, red and white,
But no such roses see I in her cheeks;
And in some perfumes is there more delight
Than in the breath that from my mistress reeks.
I love to hear her speak, yet well I know

That music hath a far more pleasing sound;
I grant I never saw a goddess go:
My mistress, when she walks, treads on the ground.
    And yet, by heaven, I think my love as rare
    As any she belied by false compare.

My mistress's eyes are not at all like the sun; coral is of a far better red than her lips; if snow is white, then her breasts are certainly not snow-white; if hairs are to be thought of as wires, hers are not golden wires but black. I have seen damask-roses, mingled red and white, but I do not see such roses in her cheeks; some perfumes give more delight than the breath that comes from her. I love to hear her speak, yet I know quite well that music sounds far better; I never saw a goddess walk, I grant, but when my mistress walks she treads on the ground. And yet I think my love as rare as any woman belied by false comparisons.

An Analysis of Sonnets 18, 29, 30, 73, and 116

Gerald Hammond

Gerald Hammond claims that the language and structure of a sonnet elicit an identifiable response in the reader. In his analysis, he pays close attention to the use of metaphors in the poems in the young man series. In the following article, Hammond analyzes Sonnets 18, 29, 30, 73, and 116—the ones that students usually study first. In Sonnet 18, the man's beauty becomes fixed in a metaphor. In Sonnet 29, the lark metaphor makes the meaning clear. In Sonnet 30, Shakespeare uses legal and financial metaphors. In Sonnet 73, the couplet controls the meaning of the previous metaphors. And in Sonnet 116, the metaphor of the North Star is central to the meaning of love.

Gerald Hammond has been a lecturer at the British Academy. He has contributed numerous articles to scholarly journals and in 1990 published *Fleeting Things: English Poets and Poems.*

SONNET 18

Sonnet 17 is a procreation sonnet still—the last of them, in fact—but now procreation has taken on the subservient role of giving support for the poet's metaphors.

That very point, the search for the best metaphor, is the subject of Sonnet 18, perhaps the best known sonnet in the [young man] sequence and probably one of the least discussed. In place of analysis one normally, and understandably, finds only praise:

> Shall I compare thee to a summer's day?
> Thou art more lovely and more temperate:
> Rough winds do shake the darling buds of May,
> 4 And summer's lease hath all too short a date;
> Sometime too hot the eye of heaven shines,

> And often is his gold complexion dimmed;
> And every fair from fair sometimes declines,
> 8   By chance or nature's changing course untrimmed:
> But thy eternal summer shall not fade,
> Nor lose possession of that fair thou ow'st,
> Nor shall death brag thou wand'rest in his shade,
> 12   When in eternal lines to time thou grow'st.
>   So long as men can breathe or eyes can see,
>   So long lives this, and this gives life to thee.

A full response to this sonnet ought to take in all the implications of the opening line. "Compare" carries the substance of all love poetry, the finding of the right image to convey the subject's beauty. The proposal is for a metaphor to be built around the image of a summer's day but it is no sooner made than it is rejected on the grounds that the young man is more lovely and more temperate than any single summer's day could be. Then the sonnet gives two separate, consecutive descriptions, the first in listing the reasons for rejecting the image actually describes various summer's days, the second describes the young man. The strange thing is that the first description is more human and attractive than the second. The clue is given in line 2: to be more lovely than a summer's day may be desirable, but to be more temperate is not. To be a darling bud of May shaken by rough winds, to be too hot and then to be dimmed is almost a summary of beauty, which depends upon chance and change; and lines 7–8 read as if they were a definition of beauty, especially when one thinks that among the possible meanings of "untrimmed" are "free of ornaments" and "with hair hanging loose":

> And every fair from fair sometimes declines,
> By chance or nature's changing course untrimmed.

In essence, part of the nature of beauty is some time to decline from beauty. But then the poet switches in the sestet to an ideal who is incapable of change—eternal summer, perpetual beauty, immortality, a never-ending poem (one sense of "eternal lines"). To be stuck in time in such a way, to be always "the same we were today or yesterday"[1] is a peculiarly poetic fate, and to have the power to do that to his subject gives the poet absolute rule.

Thus the two opposed tones inhere in this sonnet too. The reader needs to set against the grandeur of the poet's claim to

---

1. as Roman poet Ovid said

immortalise the threat which such a claim carries for its subject. The more the poet's creation gains eternal life the more the actual subject is destroyed, its extremes reduced to an unchanging permanence, so that it is fitting for Sonnet 18 to be followed by a sonnet which raises the poet to the rank of time's controller, permitting and then forbidding him to act. . . .

The great unifying concept of Sonnets 1–19 is the image of the young man as "beauty's pattern to succeeding men". In every one of the nineteen sonnets it is the poet's ideal: it opposes both the young man's wishes and time's rule, and it is ultimately achieved by turning the young man into a kind of mummy preserved in poetry. The reader's experience of the group is disturbing. He begins with remonstrations against the independence and individuality of the young man and eventually sees both of those human qualities sacrificed to poetic immortality. The text immortalises but the subtext embalms. . . .

Sonnet 29

[In several sonnets] specific metaphors are used to trouble and perplex the reader—what I shall call the obtrusive or frustrating metaphor. I ought to begin, though, by emphasising that by no means all of the sonnets in the sequence use this kind of metaphor; indeed a number, if not a great number, use metaphor to free the reader from doubt. Sonnet 29 will stand as a good example of this liberating use of metaphor. . . .

In Sonnet 29 the liberating metaphor is the lark ascending:

> When in disgrace with fortune and men's eyes
> I all alone beweep my outcast state,
> And trouble deaf heav'n with my bootless cries,
> 4   And look upon myself and curse my fate,
> Wishing me like to one more rich in hope,
> Featured like him, like him with friends possessed,
> Desiring this man's art, and that man's scope,
> 8   With what I most enjoy contented least;
> Yet in these thoughts myself almost despising,
> Haply I think on thee, and then my state,
> Like to the lark at break of day arising
> 12   From sullen earth, sings hymns at heaven's gate;
>   For thy sweet love remembered such wealth brings,
>   That then I scorn to change my state with kings.

The liberation comes partly from the metaphor's action upon the syntax of the sonnet and partly from the aptness and clarity of its image of the lark. First the syntax: the "when" which opens the sonnet leaves the reader anticipating a "then" clause which never comes; and the check at line 9, after eight lines of syntactic expectation, seems, for that line at least, to emphasise all of the negative elements of the octave. Then lines 10–12 use the image of the lark to transform all of these elements into intense celebration. Syntactically there is a release both in the fulfilment of the apparently frustrated promise of the initial "when" and in the sweep right through line 11 and into line 12 in contrast with the end-stopping of lines 1–9. In its image the metaphor provides a release from the oppressive man-centredness of the octave: a world peopled by the rich, famous, and neglected suddenly finds a new, bird's-eye perspective, and the sheer pleasure of singing for the sake of it raises the bird to the heaven's level where the man in line 3 had called fruitlessly up to it. The idea of the outcast is the same—a lark in the sky is an excellent figure of isolation—but his "state" has been transformed, so that when the couplet comes to recapitulate the change of state in the worldly terms of the octave the reader now perceives ecstatic undertones in the mundane words "wealth", "scorn", "change", "state", and "kings". The effect of the one image of the lark is total, preventing us from reading the couplet in any other way but as a triumphant vindication of the outcast poet. It would, for instance, be wrong-headed to say that it shows the poet imprisoned in the attitudes of envy ("brings such wealth"/"scorn to change my state") which had created the melodramatic self-pity of the octave. There are many such ironic ambiguities in the sonnets but here one metaphor wipes them out. In the metaphor's clarity of purpose Sonnet 29 is unusual. . . .

SONNET 30

The argument of this article is that the reader's experience of the sonnets is intimately bound up with his response to individual metaphors. A metaphor which is obtrusive or vague may well undermine, or at least obscure, a sonnet's literal statement. That literal statement will not usually be abandoned but it will have to co-exist with a potentially frustrating metaphoric competition. In some sonnets, though, the competition between metaphor and statement is a sustaining, not frustrating, element. An example is Sonnet 30 which has one of the most exhaustive metaphors in the sonnets:

When to the sessions of sweet silent thought

> I summon up remembrance of things past,
> I sigh the lack of many a thing I sought,
> 4   And with old woes new wail my dear time's waste.
> Then can I drown an eye, unused to flow,
> For precious friends hid in death's dateless night,
> And weep afresh love's long since cancelled woe,
> 8   And moan th' expense of many a vanished sight.
> Then can I grieve at grievances foregone,
> And heavily from woe to woe tell o'er
> The sad account of fore-bemoaned moan,
> 12   Which I new pay as if not paid before.
>   But if the while I think on thee, dear friend,
>   All losses are restored, and sorrows end.

Coldly abstracted Sonnet 30 says the following: "When I meditate I remember dead friends whom I have long since ceased mourning over. I feel their loss anew until I think of you; with that thought I cease grieving at their loss." That statement pays a great tribute to the power of the young man but it also has strong negative, reductive undertones which are only held in check by the distance between the sonnet's statement and the metaphor it uses. The metaphor is, of course, a legal/financial one, beginning at "sessions" and continuing through "summon up", "precious", "cancelled", "expense", "tell o'er", "account", "pay" and "paid", to "losses are restored". Added to those obvious images there is a strain of words which carry secondary legal/financial senses: "lack", "dear", "waste", "unused", "dateless", "foregone", and "dear" again in the couplet. Nonetheless I can sympathise, if not agree, with Martin Seymour-Smith's judgement that the legal metaphor is "unobtrusive", largely because it has to compete with another line of imagery, the poet's sorrow: "sigh", "old woes", "new wail", "drown an eye", "unused to flow", "weep afresh", "moan", "grieve at grievances", "heavily", "from woe to woe", "sad", "fore-bemoaned moan", and "sorrows". I call this a line of imagery because it does not quite have the standing of a metaphor; elements of it are metaphorical, but the reader's vision is on sighs and tears—a literal sadness opposed to a figurative financial court. And what prevents the literal and the figurative from overcoming each other is the surprising degree to which they fail to interact. Put simply, the part of the mind which sees Thought presiding over his court and summoning witnesses, the cancelling of debts and the spending of money, will not directly, or even indirectly, relate these images to sighs and tears.

There must, of course, be some kind of fusion at work,

otherwise the sonnet would be merely ludicrous. . . . I believe that the fusion comes in the second quatrain, where the death of friends which causes the poet's literal sorrow is related to the figurative cancelling of debts and spending of money. But it is important to emphasise that this is a shadowy fusion. "Dateless" has its double reference—death has no end, like a lease which has no fixed term—but neither it nor the rest of the metaphor can be absorbed into the sonnet's statement. . . . Here the death of friends can not be so conveniently labelled. It exists, of course, as a poetic subject, but not normally as a subject, let alone a vehicle, for love poetry, one of whose conventional metaphors is the legal/financial. In essence Sonnet 30 preserves the balance between subject and metaphor, permitting the reader neither to turn it into the reductive statement "you are all my dead friends", nor to read it as the involved love conceit which so much of its language points toward. . . .

SONNET 73

Sonnets 71 and 72 fix on the young man's actions in an imagined future after the poet's death. The apparent nearness of this event prepares the way for the much celebrated Sonnet 73, in which the poet uses three successive metaphors, one to a quatrain, in order to portray his developing old age and imminent death:

> That time of year thou mayst in me behold,
> When yellow leaves, or none, or few, do hang
> Upon those boughs which shake against the cold,
> 4 Bare ruined choirs, where late the sweet birds sang.
> In me thou seest the twilight of such day,
> As after sunset fadeth in the west,
> Which by and by black night doth take away,
> 8 Death's second self, that seals up all in rest.
> In me thou seest the glowing of such fire,
> That on the ashes of his youth doth lie,
> As the death-bed whereon it must expire,
> 12 Consumed with that which it was nourished by.
> This thou perceiv'st, which makes thy love more strong,
> To love that well which thou must leave ere long.

This sonnet is so attractive in its metaphoric structure that it has often been cited as the archetypal Shakespearean sonnet, what Alden[2] called "the finest example of the Shakespearean mode". It may be archetypal in the terms of the ghostly

2. critic R.M.

4:4:4:2 pattern which underlies this kind of sonnet but it actually represents one of the less frequent Shakespearean sonnet structures. Most critical comment on it has understandably concentrated on its metaphoric process—the way in which it helps enact the ageing of the man it describes—but behind the narrowing down from year to day to glowing embers the sonnet does something more, separate from, and to an extent contrary to, its metaphors. This something else is contained in the sonnet's verbs. In the opening line "thou mayst in me behold" is not likely to be interpreted by the reader as anything other than a general statement—an interpretation supported by the breadth of the metaphor which follows. In other words, the reader feels as much addressed as the young man, if not more so; and he therefore takes the statement as the poet's actual opinion of himself. In the second and third quatrains "thou seest" modifies the reader's position only a little. The absence of the auxiliary "may" locates the sonnet as more particularly an address to the young man, but it remains one which the reader can share, as we all share supposedly intimate poems which, while they address themselves to a lover, describe the poet's general state. In the couplet, though, the reader is forced out of the address by the specificity of "this thou perceiv'st"; also, the narrowness of "perceive" conveys, in retrospect, a stronger and more confined sense into the earlier verbs of "beholding" and "seeing", as if to say "these metaphors, so graphically describing my decline, are the way you see me". I do not mean by this that the poet does not imagine himself as old, but that by the verb "perceive" he demonstrates his awareness of the young man's attitude to his ageing: the three times repeated "in me" carries the implication that this is not the whole truth about the poet, only a part of the truth which the young man extracts and which ignores a lot. The couplet is pregnant with the irony of prospective legatees at the death beds of rich relatives, the difference in values between the young man and the poet coming in the unexpected "which thou must leave". Ingram[3] and Redpath[4] note the incongruity of the live leaving the dead by glossing "leave" as "forgo", not "depart from", but following Sonnets 71 and 72, where it is the young man's version of the relationship, conditioned by the world's demands, which will survive as its record, this

3. critic W.G.   4. critic Theodore

reversal of the natural order embodies the different values of the two men. In the young man's view even the most final and unavoidable of partings—the poet's death—is transformed into an act of will on his own part. . . .

SONNET 116

Sonnet 115's confusion spreads from an analytic, and potentially cynical, mind's attempts to use the word "now"—to be certain about the present. In apparently complete contrast Sonnet 116 forgets analysis and cynicism, and irresistibly asserts one way to be certain about the present:

> Let me not to the marriage of true minds
> Admit impediments. Love is not love
> Which alters when it alteration finds,
> 4 Or bends with the remover to remove.
> O no, it is an ever-fixed mark
> That looks on tempests and is never shaken;
> It is the star to every wandering bark,
> 8 Whose worth's unknown, although his height be taken.
> Love's not time's fool, though rosy lips and cheeks
> Within his bending sickle's compass come.
> Love alters not with his brief hours and weeks,
> 12 But bears it out even to the edge of doom.
>> If this be error and upon me proved,
>> I never writ, nor no man ever loved.

. . . In rhythm, syntax, verb tense, and poetic structure, Sonnet 115 encourages the reader to consider and reconsider what is being, and what has been, said. This sonnet does the opposite, its high monotone leading the reader unthinkingly through a series of statements about love: love is not, love is, love's not, love alters not, but love bears it out. The primacy of this idea of defining love can be measured by the reader's reaction to lines 7–8:

> It is the star to every wandering bark,
> Whose worth's unknown . . .

In the process of reading most Shakespearean sonnets the reader might be tempted to take the first half of line 8 as part of the description of the "bark", as in normal English prose syntax; or at the least he would hold in parallel the two possibilities that it refers back either to "bark" or to "star". But here there can be no possible doubt that the proper antecedent is neither "bark" nor "star", but the "it" which begins line 7, love itself.

The contrast with Sonnet 115 is not only formal; in effect

116 provides an answer to the complexities of its predecessor. It proposes a love which exists in an unchanging present, impervious to time's millioned accidents. "Love's not time's fool" is a peculiarly oblique contrast to the image of reckoning time whose accidents "Creep in 'twixt vows, and change decrees of kings", not least because here time is presented as a much more regal figure, despite the overall assertion that his rule can be resisted. This, I think, gives a clue to the ultimate insubstantiality of the sonnet....

The vagueness is justified because the sonnet's declared subject is nonexistent except in the person of the poet himself. "Love is not love which ..." is the start of a definition which eventually excludes all action, identity, and knowledge. This love fails to respond to human movement in the first quatrain, resists figuratively even the sea's movement in the second, and, ultimately, time's sickle in the third. Its nature is that of the North Star's, the one fixed point in a turning world. But its chief characteristic is its isolation. Unlike, for example, Donne's[5] unique lovers, this love is a solitary figure. The world is both literally and figuratively in contrast with it, in a state of error—"... alteration ... remover ... tempests ... wandering bark ... time's fool ... rosy lips and cheeks ... brief hours and weeks". That this love is the poet is borne upon the reader by the sonnet's framing, which is essentially defensive. The couplet, as many commentators have noted, is pure illogicality, but nonetheless fitting in that it asserts without possibility of refutation the truth of the poet's description of love; but what they fail to bring out is that it returns the sonnet to the vulnerability of the opening lines. "I never writ, nor no man ever loved", in itself a breathtakingly pompous parallel, is made doubly so in its posing as the logical consequence to the poet's being in error. What prevents it from being experienced like that, however, is the reader's sense of the poet's defensiveness from the opening of the sonnet. "Let me not to the marriage of true minds / Admit impediments" is not quite so trouble-free a request as editors seem to imply. They feel duty bound to note, although all readers are certain to pick it up, its echoing of the marriage service, but they largely ignore the reader's real problem which is to assess whether or not the poet is one of the "marriage" partners. It is at least possible

5. poet John

that the prayer book echo points to his not being, since the call to admit impediment is made to the other members of the congregation, not the actual couple. This response obviously makes "marriage of true minds" an ironic phrase, and it also points clearly towards the exclusion and exclusivity of the rest of the first quatrain:

> Love is not love
> Which alters when it alteration finds,
> Or bends with the remover to remove.

"Alteration" and "remover" are primarily words to describe infidelity, and the metaphoric image of the quatrain becomes that of a member of the congregation at a wedding who could, but out of greater love will not give cause or just impediment. If, though, the reader is not prepared to treat "marriage of true minds" ironically, seeing instead the poet as one of the married pair, then he has to find a way of coping with the marriage in the context of alteration and removal which the rest of the quatrain insists upon. The only way is to drive back into the opening lines the sense that the poet will not be the one to admit impediments, but his partner will: a sense reinforced by the rest of the sonnet's emphasis on images of uniqueness and isolation.

"Love's not time's fool" is an unexpected and exciting expansion of the sonnet's reference, presenting the poet as not only a unique lover, but as a unique man, whose vision makes his life independent of time's rule. As a personal vision it seems one way out of the dilemma of a world governed by time.

Dramatic Shifts in Emphasis Make Sonnet 73 an Effective Poem

Stephen Booth

Stephen Booth asserts that Shakespeare's sonnets are unique because the relationships in them are "in flux"; thoughts, images, and grammatical structures flow through the poems with surprising shifts. Booth analyzes Sonnet 73, claiming that the poem presents three images. Booth concludes that the significance of the images diminishes as the importance of the poem's idea increases. Then, in the couplet, another shift occurs when the person spoken to replaces the speaker, a change that causes the reader to reexamine the previous lines.

Stephen Booth has taught English at the University of California at Berkeley. He has both written about and edited a collection of Shakespeare's sonnets and is the author of a book on Shakespeare's tragedies.

The following attempt at tracing a reader's mind through sonnet 73 will illustrate the shifting of contexts and the several other qualities whose effects are analogous to it.

Line 1 introduces and relates four elements: a season, the speaker, the opportunity to behold, and a beholder—*That time of year thou mayst in me behold*. The first two of these elements provide the substance of line 2, which straightforwardly identifies the season whose likeness is visible in the speaker: *When yellow leaves, or none, or few, do hang*. The reader is the beholder as he goes through the poem, and this line is calculated to be looked at quickly and passed over. It shows the reader what the demonstrative, *that*, in line 1 was pointing to, and, since it answers a question left over from line 1, it leads the reader on.... The reader is given the de-

Excerpted from *An Essay on Shakespeare's Sonnets* by Stephen Booth (New Haven, CT: Yale University Press, 1969). Copyright 1969 by Yale University. Reprinted by permission of the publisher.

sire to see what season *that* season is. This much Shakespeare can literally show him. Logically, the proposition, "I personate Autumn," is a conceit. . . .

THE ORDER OF AUTUMN

The order of *yellow leaves, none,* and *few* is not at all what might be expected. To begin with, the sequence does not follow the sequence of nature: in nature there are yellow leaves first, then few, then none. As it is, this list does not flow into the reader's mind as it would if it came to him neatly generalized in almanac order. At a given moment in autumn an actual beholder of trees shifts his eyes, turns his head, looks around, and sees some trees with full yellowed foliage, some bare, and some with a few leaves; the same variation is likely among the various branches of a single tree. Reading this line is like looking at nature unmethodized. I am not saying that the action of reading the line suggests to its reader the action of looking at a tree or any other such anamorphous claptrap. I do say that reading this line *is* an action, that the reader is active. The reading of the line demands that the reader perform the intellectual action of looking, seeing, and grasping what he perceives. . . .

The mind of a reader of line 2 of sonnet 73 is in motion. His mind does not puzzle as it does when it tries to understand an obscure line, but neither does it receive the stimuli of the poem passively. The sonnets are not what we ordinarily call hard poems, nor are they easy ones. They are uneasy: the relationships within the poems are in flux and the reader's mind is too. People are always saying that the sonnets are unique. They are. . . .

To demonstrate, I will return in somewhat less detail to sonnet 73:

> That time of year thou mayst in me behold
> When yellow leaves, or none, or few, do hang
> Upon those boughs which shake against the cold,
> Bare ruined choirs[1] where late the sweet birds sang.
> In me thou seest the twilight of such day
> As after sunset fadeth in the west,
> Which by and by black night doth take away,
> Death's second self that seals up[2] all in rest.
> In me thou seest the glowing of such fire
> That on the ashes of his youth doth lie,

---

1. that part of a cathedral in which services are conducted   2. concludes

As the deathbed whereon it must expire,
Consumed with that which it was nourished by.
   This thou perceiv'st, which makes thy love more strong,
   To love that well which thou must leave ere long.

PROGRESSIONS IN THE QUATRAINS

The artificial order of this sonnet is particularly insistent: there are three quatrains, one each for the tree, twilight, and fire; each quatrain is a single sentence; and the couplet is a fourth and summary sentence. The formal identity of the three quatrains is reinforced substantially and syntactically: the three quatrains compare the speaker to a tree, twilight, and fire, respectively; each quatrain is a single sentence; and the first lines of the second and the third quatrains echo line 1.

Moreover, there are several coexistent progressions in the quatrains. Time is measured in progressively smaller units: a season of a year, a part of a day, and the last moments of the hour or so that a fire burns. Color grows increasingly intense: yellow leaves, twilight after sunset, fire. Light grows dimmer: daylight (presumably) in quatrain one, twilight, night; space constricts from the cold windy first quatrain to the hot suffocating grave of ashes in the third. In a progression concurrent with all these the metaphors give up an increasingly larger percentage of each succeeding quatrain to the abstract subject of the sonnet, human mortality. In the first quatrain the reader's need to see the likeness between autumn and the speaker is not urgent; line 1 makes the connection but, except for suggestions—first of aged human limbs in the *boughs which shake against the cold* and then of the universality of mutability[3] in the fusion of substances that follows—the first quatrain focuses its reader's attention on the autumn scene rather than on the speaker. The progression toward the dominance of the tenor[4] begins in quatrain 2, where *twilight* is a step closer than *boughs* had been to being personified.[5] The suggestion of physical abduction latent in the phrasing of *black night doth take away* asserts itself in the apposition of *Death's second self to black night;* because death and its traditional second self, sleep, pertain

3. the idea that change and alteration are widespread and inevitable   4. flow of the main argument   5. Boughs are like human arms, and both boughs and arms can shake. Shaking *against* the cold suggests that the shaker feels cold and thus goes some way toward presenting the reader with a solid equation between a leafless tree and an aging man, but the image of a tree never crystallizes in the poem, and the boughs are immediately equated with the also inanimate *ruined choirs*.

only to animate objects, human mortality is much more evidently inherent in the metaphor of quatrain 2 than it was in that of quatrain 1. By the end of the third quatrain the metaphor is all but dwarfed by its tenor: after the introduction of the *fire* and its ashes comes explicit personification in *his youth* and *deathbed.* The tenor so completely emerges from the metaphor that, although the shift in *form* between the third quatrain and the couplet is, as usual, pronounced, the reader accepts the unadorned statement of the couplet with no sense that the *mode* of the poem has shifted from exemplum to moral.

All of these orderly progressions go to reinforce the formal order of the three-quatrain pattern. However, as the formal break between the third quatrain and the couplet is countered by the gentleness of the modulation between the three exempla and the moral, so in the poem as a whole the three-quatrain pattern and the progressions that support it are so offset by other factors that the poem provides the artistic security and stability of predictable pattern without allowing its reader the intellectual repose that predictability can entail. A principal factor in offsetting the potential liabilities of regularity is the numerousness of the different progressions within the pattern of quatrains. The progressions are consistent with one another and with the nature of the three metaphors, but they are not mechanically parallel and do not lump together in the mind: the time units get smaller; the speaker looms larger; the color gets brighter; the light gets dimmer; the temperature gets hotter. . . .

PROGRESSION IN QUATRAINS 2 AND 3

In the first lines of quatrain 2, the precise meaning of *twilight of such day* shifts as the lines are read. Meeting *twilight of* a reader expects *day* because the possessive is ordinarily pertinent only to *day*; he therefore takes something like the meaning "twilight of such *a* day" from *twilight of such day.* The next line begins with the word *as,* which, in the usual pattern of the language, is a sign to the reader that the clause it introduces will tell him about the departed day whose twilight is under discussion. Such a clause can be reasonably expected to be in the past tense. The clause actually introduced by *As* is not in the past tense and is not the expected parenthetical identification of the day in question: *As after sunset fadeth in the west.* The modifying clause acts upon both *day* and *twilight* and effectively makes the reader understand *twilight of such day* as "what little is left of the day." Although it is unfulfilled, the syntactical promise in *As* of defining detail to follow is sufficient in itself to give the reader a sense that the metaphor has been precisely established. Weighing against that sense of sureness is the action of the line that actually follows *As.* It pushes forward in the present tense and makes the reader participate in little in a mutability in the lines themselves that seems so powerful it cannot be stopped even for the moment it would take to establish a definition.

In the next lines the reader's mind is again in motion. *Night*, in the context of *twilight*, is expected, but here *night* is called *Death's second self*. Since *black night* suggests a ghostly figure capable of abducting the twilight, the equation with death is easy to accept. However, *Death's second self* suggests the traditional epithet for sleep, "the younger brother of Death." The suggestion of sleep inherent in the epithet is then confirmed by the rest of the line: *that seals up all in rest.* Night and sleep are closely related concepts, and there is nothing startling about the mention of one leading to the mention of the other. Here, however, the reader's mind must act upon the lines, adjusting its understanding as the idea of night fuses into, and at last is almost lost in, the idea of sleep, which, in *lie* and *deathbed,* is still dimly present in the next quatrain.

Another kind of demand for mental activity is put upon the reader by the parallelism between the second and third quatrains. Except for the replacement in line 9 of *glowing* and *fire* for *twilight* and *day* in line 5, the first lines of the two quatrains are identical. The reader is prepared to see line 10 continue the parallelism. The explanation demanded by *such* in *of such day* is introduced by *as*; the reader, set firmly in a repeating pattern, expects line 10 to begin as line 6 had. Instead of "*As* on the ashes of his youth doth lie," the line is "*That* on the ashes of his youth doth lie." Then, reconciled to the miniscule disappointment of the broken pattern, the reader meets *As*, the word expected at the beginning of line 10, in the same position but with a different syntactical function in line 11: *As the deathbed whereon it must expire.* As he reads quatrain 3 a reader's mind recognizes a repeating pattern, adjusts to a break in it, and then must accept a factor in the original pattern used randomly.

REVERSAL IN THE COUPLET

Something of the same sort happens in the couplet where the verb *leave* is a substantially irrelevant, almost purely phonetic, echo of the *leaves* at the beginning of the poem:

> This thou perceiv'st, which makes thy love more strong,
> To love that well which thou must leave ere long.

The couplet requires further adjustment of the pattern in which the reader conceives relationship in the poem. The couplet is in perfect accord with the substance of the poem. Moreover, it begins (*This thou perceiv'st*) like the three previous formal units, each of which introduces its metaphor with a statement that what follows is to be seen in the speaker. The construction of the final clause of the poem, however, contradicts the pattern for syntactically secondary action in the poem. The person to whom the poem is addressed has been the actor in the main clause of each sentence, but the bulk of each of the quatrains is devoted to metaphoric statements of the impending departure of the speaker. Here, in *which thou must leave ere long*, the action is stated in reverse. The beholder is the actor; now the beholder must leave the speaker. The reader has no difficulty in understanding the line. He simply understands *leave* as "give up" or "lose." Even so, the reversal of the previous action is effective. It brings the threat of mortality closer to the beholder, completing the reader's sense that mutability is universal. More importantly, the change itself and the reader's need to follow it provide one more demand for the reader's activity, commitment, and participation in the process of the poem.

Shakespeare's Sonnets Imitate and Satirize Earlier Sonnets

Katharine M. Wilson

Katharine M. Wilson argues that Shakespeare wrote his sonnets in the context of his times. He wrote when poets were beginning to abandon the use of flowery and ornate rhetoric in favor of a plainer, more natural style. Familiar with the ornate poetic devices of the old but preferring the plainer language of the new, Shakespeare imitated and exaggerated ornate language to promote the new, according to Wilson. To support her argument, Wilson compares Shakespeare's sonnets with sonnets from poets who preceded Shakespeare. Wilson presents six sonnets—18, 29, 30, 73, 116, and 130—and follows each with poems she thinks Shakespeare imitated.

Katharine M. Wilson received her education at Cambridge University. A writer, she published a collection of essays, *Mint Sauce*, in 1927. She has also published critical works on poetry, a children's book, and a study of Keats, as well as her own poetry.

[In the latter half of Queen Elizabeth's reign] the ideal of poetry as 'sugared', as rhetoric, as beautiful artifact was [exhausted]. We can still see it in their books of rhetoric and the art of poetry, but the new poets had grown out of it. Plain speech began to win their approval, and the beginnings of an ideal of truth to nature. This new attitude dates from precisely the sonnet period, the 1590s. . . . Shakespeare considered the question in *Love's Labours Lost*, and . . . in *Romeo and Juliet* he plays with both modes of expression, setting one against the other for dramatic purposes, the sugared style as contrast for the plain speech of real love. I also suggest that he made a considered choice. He began in the old

Excerpted from *Shakespeare's Sugared Sonnets* by Katharine M. Wilson (New York: Barnes & Noble, 1974), by courtesy of the author's estate.

style and moved into the new, although from the first his own finest imaginings, as we see them, tended to be in the new style. Thus *Venus and Adonis* is ornate, but the imagery often shows a modern fidelity to the thing seen, and this we also find in his earliest plays. Indeed this sort of imaginative truth possibly has a place in all great narrative poetry; it is certainly there in both Homer and [Geoffrey] Chaucer. Nevertheless there are fashions, and about this time a shift occurred from court artifice to truth to nature. That Shakespeare posed the question of ornate or plain speech in the theatre shows that it was not just a scholar's or a poet's problem. *Love's Labours Lost* presupposes cultured young men ready for the new approach, or at least for criticism of the old. There is a climate favouring a new approach to the sonnet.

This is the context in which Shakespeare wrote his sonnet sequence.... Shakespeare must have had the cadences, imagery and ideas of his predecessors in his mind as he wrote. He used the same or similar tunes and the same imagery and conceits as the other sonneteers, to pay the same flattering and devoted attention, but to a man, not a woman. Apart from this he differed from them only by beginning his sonnet sequence with a section of seventeen sonnets each coming to an identical and ridiculous climax in the couplet, begging his friend to marry and that for the most fantastic of reasons, and by reserving the more vituperative outpourings of sonnet tradition for a woman. That is to say he reduced the whole thing to the absurd.

Nothing is more difficult than to prove a joke, for the only proof is to be surprised into laughter by it....

SONNET 18

Shall I compare thee to a summer's day?
Thou art more lovely and more temperate:
Rough winds do shake the darling buds of May,
And summer's lease hath all too short a date:
Sometime too hot the eye of heaven[1] shines,
And often is his gold complexion dimmed,
And every fair from fair sometime declines,
By chance, or nature's changing course untrimmed:[2]
But thy eternal summer shall not fade,
Nor lose possession of that fair thou owest,[3]
Nor shall death brag thou wanderest in his shade,
When in eternal lines to time thou growest,

1. the sun 2. shorn of beauty 3. beauty you possess

So long as men can breathe or eyes can see,
So long lives this, and this gives life to thee.

Sonnet 18 begins the new section that lasts till sonnet 32. It
was skilfully prepared for by stepping up the power of time,
and then introducing the poet's verse as a defence. In sonnet
17 Shakespeare said he would preserve his friend in rhyme,
and here he considers what he should say about him. The
sonnet springs very obviously out of his reading of Spenser[4]
who wrote in sonnet IX,

Long-while I sought to what I might compare
Those powerful eyes, which lighté my dark sprite,
Yet find I nought on earth to which I dare
Resemble the image of their goodly light.
Not to the sun: for they do shine by night.

So on he goes, 'Not to the moon . . .' giving a line to each of
his eight suggestions. He also aims to 'eternise' her virtues
in sonnet LXXV. It is just possible that Spenser's sonnet
XXVII, where he says his love 'Shall doff her flesh's borrowed fair attire' may have suggested Shakespeare's 'lose
possession of that fair thou owest'. . . .

SONNET 29

When in disgrace with fortune and men's eyes,
I all alone beweep my outcast state,
And trouble deaf heaven with my bootless[5] cries,
And look upon myself and curse my fate.
Wishing me like to one more rich in hope,
Featured like him, like him with friends possessed,
Desiring this man's art, and that man's scope,
With what I most enjoy contented least,
Yet in these thoughts myself almost despising,
Haply I think on thee, and then my state,
(Like to the lark at break of day arising)
From sullen earth sings hymns at heaven's gate,
    For thy sweet love remembered such wealth brings,
    That then I scorn to change my state with kings.

That this is parody we could not doubt. To be in disgrace with
fortune in sonnet language is to be out of favour with one's
lady, and to be this is to be in disgrace with her eyes. The two
statements mean the same thing. Shakespeare's substituting
'men's eyes' for 'lady's eyes' could be only parody. Having
dealt with this situation translated into social terms in his last
sonnet, Shakespeare treats it over-emotionally in this, or in

4. Edmund   5. vain

other words he behaves as the lover does in his situation. He cries to heaven, he curses his fate, he wishes he had every good fortune, and he makes sure we take it as good fortune in the world, not in the usual sonnet sense. When 'almost despising' himself (why 'almost'?) he just happens ('haply') to think of his friend, and suddenly, instead of praying in despair, he is like a lark singing at 'heaven's gate'.

All this is hysterical, but it is not difficult to find passages to justify the parody, and from many poets. The fortune, the stars, the disgrace, the lady's eyes—all have their antecedents. And the way these are combined in the same sonnets, and seem to belong together is impressive. Sidney[6] in sonnet LXIV writes,

> Let fortune lay on me her worst disgrace.
> Let folk o'ercharged with brain against me cry,
> Let clouds be dim, my fate bereaves mine eyes,
> Let me no steps but of lost labour try,
> Let all the earth in scorn recount my race.

He asks nothing at all

> But that which once may win thy cruel heart,
> Thou art my wit; and thou my virtue art.

And in LXVI he says that in spite of all, there is one hope,

> Stella's eyes[7] sent to me the beams of bliss.

Constable[8] complains of his disgrace in decade 5, sonnet II;

> I do not now complain of my disgrace,
> Oh cruel fair one, fair with cruel crossed:
> Nor of the hour, season, time nor place.

And Daniel[9] in sonnet XX says,

> This is her laurel and her triumph's prize,
> To tread me down with foot of her disgrace:
> Whilst I did build my fortune in her eyes.

Sonnet 30, as already suggested, mocks by singing Constable's tune. Here are grand abstract nouns—'sessions of sweet, silent thought', 'remembrance of things past'. His precious friends are hid in 'death's dateless night'. All the sorrows of the past combine with 'time's waste' in the present and lead to the poet grieving at 'grievances foregone' and 'heavily' telling over 'The sad account of fore-bemoaned moan'. After this full and mournful dignity, comes the familiar speech, dear friend of every day. When Shakespeare

6. Sir Philip   7. Sidney addressed his sonnets to a beautiful woman he called Stella.
8. Henry, who addressed his sonnets to Diana   9. Samuel, who wrote sonnets to Delia

thinks of him 'all losses are restored', 'death's dateless night' quite forgot, all 'sorrows end'. We have come to expect this sudden bathos in the couplet, and if I may say so, putting everything in the stew.

SONNET 30

When to the sessions[10] of sweet silent thought,
I summon up remembrance of things past,
I sigh the lack of many a thing I sought,
And with old woes new wail my dear time's waste:
Then can I drown an eye (unused to flow)
For precious friends hid in death's dateless[11] night,
And weep afresh love's long since cancelled woe,
And moan the expense[12] of many a vanished sight.
Then can I grieve at grievances foregone,[13]
And heavily from woe to woe tell o'er
The sad account of fore-bemoaned moan,
Which I new pay as if not paid before.
        But if the while I think on thee (dear friend)
        All losses are restored, and sorrows end.

The punning has been pointed out by Professor Mahood. The play on 'dear', 'precious', 'cancelled', 'expense', 'tell', 'account', 'pay', 'paid', 'dear', 'foregone' meaning 'repudiated and forgotten' as well as just having happened—these give comic glints in the richly toned verse.

Daniel's sonnet XXV, it should be noted, provides phrases for sonnets 29, 30 and 31. It begins,

Reign in my thoughts fair hand, sweet eye, rare voice.

He calls them his 'heart's triumvirate' and says that

    Whilst they strive which shall be lord of all,
All my poor life by them is trodden down:
They all erect their trophies on my fall.

    .   .   .   .   .   .

When back I look, I sigh my freedom past,
And wail the state wherein I present stand.

These lines are echoed in sonnet 31 by 'there reigns love', 'all love's loving parts', 'the trophies of my lovers gone'. Incidentally, in sonnet X Daniel says that he 'serves a trophy to her conquering eyes'. The last two lines of my quotation give the theme of 30, which indeed elaborates it. 'Wail the state' is echoed in the second line of 29 in 'beweep my outcast state'.

What sonnet 30 does with emotion, 31 does with an ingenious play of mind. . . .

10. sittings of a law court   11. everlasting   12. waste   13. past

SONNET 73

In sonnet 73 Shakespeare again writes on approaching death, but in a different mood. We should not forget that he was a young man when he wrote it.

> That time of year thou mayst in me behold,
> When yellow leaves, or none, or few do hang
> Upon those boughs which shake against the cold,
> Bare ruined choirs,[14] where late the sweet birds sang.
> In me thou seest the twilight of such day,
> As after sunset fadeth in the west,
> Which by and by black night doth take away,
> Death's second self that seals up[15] all in rest.
> In me thou seest the glowing of such fire,
> That on the ashes of his youth doth lie,
> As the death-bed, whereon it must expire,
> Consumed with that which it was nourished by.
>   This thou perceiv'st, which makes thy love more strong,
>   To love that well, which thou must leave ere long.

Sonneteers ask their ladies to love while it is summer before winter comes, the argument for love lying in the short time it can last. Shakespeare has gone one better. He says it is already winter with him. He is at death's door. His time is *very* short. Since you can see this, he tells his friend, you should love me more.

Some of the credit for this sonnet must go to Daniel, who in sonnet XXXII combines the arguments in the first two quatrains, asking Delia to love while it is summer and in the morning before night comes, and in sonnet XXXIV where he requests her to read his verse on her

> When winter snows upon thy golden hairs,
> And frost of age hath nipped thy flowers near:
> When dark shall seem thy day that never clears,
> And all lies withered that was held so dear.

Barnes[16] in sonnet LIX brings together

> The leafless branches of the lifeless boughs
> Carve winter's outrage in their withered barks.

and

> The withered wrinkles in my careful brows.

And although he is saying something different, Constable in decade 6, sonnet VI may have contributed to the imagery in the third quatrain, where he refers to

14. the part of a cathedral in which the services are conducted 15. concludes
16. poet Barnabe

Thy beauty so, the brightest living flame,
Wrapped in my cloudy heart by winter pressed.

He exclaims,

Oh that my heart might still contain that fire,

.   .   .   .   .   .

For as the fire through freezing clouds doth break,
So, not myself, but thou in me would speak.

The fire is linked with frost and winter, although it is the sun
that Constable is writing about. His imagery, however, relat-
ing fire with winter may have been in Shakespeare's mind.
But all these are common sonnet images. Shakespeare has
geared the 'bare ruined choirs', the twilight and the ashes to
death and created the most unforgettable of all the sonnets,
ridiculous only in the implication that the strength of love is
in inverse ratio to the length of time remaining for it, or in
this being used as a relevant argument for love. . . .

SONNET 116

Let me not to the marriage of true minds
Admit impediments, love is not love
Which alters when it alteration finds,
Or bends with the remover to remove.[17]
Oh no, it is an ever fixed mark
That looks on tempests and is never shaken;
It is the star to every wandering bark,
Whose worth's unknown, although his height be taken.
Love's not time's fool,[18] though rosy lips and cheeks
Within his bending sickle's compass come,
Love alters not with his brief hours and weeks,
But bears it out even to the edge of doom:[19]
  If this be error and upon me proved,
  I never writ, nor no man ever loved.

Taken seriously this sonnet has given many readers a moving experience. It is perfectly said. But not only is the tone
sarcastic, the form of the sentences suggests doubt. It begins
with the church declaration of marriage banns, where anyone who knows 'just cause or impediment' is asked to come
forward now and say so. Shakespeare takes the position of
one considering the matter, who is not going to admit impediment. 'Let me not' is the opening of the debater making
a point. The first point is that love which alters 'when it alteration finds' is not love. This is a backhanded admission
that some love does alter. 'Oh no,' Shakespeare continues.

17. wishes to change when the loved one is inconstant   18. mocked by time
19. doomsday

The words imply that he has been contradicted, or envisages a contradiction. But he asserts emphatically that love is an 'ever-fixed mark' like a lighthouse steady in tempest, or the lodestar, whose value is mysterious beyond knowledge, although mathematicians calculate its height. 'Love is not time's fool' he emphasises, perhaps implying that someone has said it is. Love lasts till the day of judgement. Shakespeare seems to be protesting too much. Then finally, on any reading the couplet makes one feel uneasy about its sincerity. It is a trite commonplace.

Let me now look at Shakespeare's evidence. Spenser's sonnet XXXIV is very much to the point:

> Like as a ship that through the ocean wide,
> By conduct of some star doth make her way.
> When as a storm hath dimmed her trusty guide.
> Out of her course doth wander far astray:
> So I whose star, that wont with her bright ray,
> Me to direct, with clouds is overcast,
> Do wander now in darkness and dismay,
> Through hidden perils round about me plast.
> Yet hope I well, that when this storm is past
> My Helice the lodestar of my life
> Will shine again, and look on me at last,
> With lovely light to clear my cloudy grief,
> Till then I wander careful comfortless,
> In secret sorrow and sad pensiveness.

With this in mind Shakespeare can support himself in doubt. 'Oh no, love is this star, this light in the storm'. Greville[20] in sonnet LXXXVI says:

> Love is the peace whereto all thoughts do strive,
> Done and begun with all our powers in one;
> The first and last in us that is alive,
> End of the good and therewith pleased alone.
>
> .   .   .   .
>
> Constant, because it sees no cause to vary,
> A quintessence[21] of passions overthrown,
> Raised above all that change of objects carry,
> A nature by no other nature known;
> For glory's of eternity a frame,
> That by all bodies else obscures her name.

Oh no, love is this fixed mark, 'whereto all thoughts do strive'. Here is love with 'no cause to vary', 'End of the good', the moral philosopher's goal. Or Shakespeare may find support in Surrey, who makes an impassioned statement in son-

20. Sir Fulke   21. the pure essence

net XII of Tottel[22]:

> Set me whereas the sun doth parch the green,
> Or where his beams do not dissolve the ice:
> In temperate heat where he is felt and seen:
> In presence pressed of people mad or wise.
> Set me in high, or yet in low degree:
> In longest night, or in the shortest day:
> In clearest sky, or where clouds thickest be:
> In lusty youth, or when my hairs are gray.
> Set me in heaven, in earth, or else in hell,
> In hill, or dale, or in the foaming flood:
> Thrall, or at large, alive where so I dwell:
> Hers will I be, and only with this thought
> Content myself, although my chance be nought.

All sonneteers illustrate this constancy in one form or another, no matter what they suffer from the disdain and discouragement they receive. And even if we remember such apostate sonneteers as Wyatt,[23] we can say he made himself notorious merely by 'altering' because of his lady's attitude.

What we could call 'external' proof of the ironic character of Shakespeare's sonnet can be seen in that not only the one immediately preceding, but the series of sonnets immediately following, present love as far from being fixed and constant. That this sonnet appears precisely in this place suggests irony. . . .

SONNET 130

Those on the dark lady already strike many readers as unconvincing; taken seriously, they may provide a good opening. They can hardly have been written to a woman in compliment, and unless one approaches them already convinced, it is difficult to believe that they could have been written about a real woman. Indeed, nothing is easier than to show they are parodies. Some can even be shown to have a particular sonnet in view, and in general their meaning is best unlocked with this key.

There can be no mistake about this:

> My mistress' eyes are nothing like the sun,
> Coral is far more red, than her lips red,
> If snow be white, why then her breasts are dun:
> If hairs be wires, black wires grow on her head:
> I have seen roses damasked,[24] red and white,
> But no such roses see I in her cheeks,

---

22. *Tottel's Miscellany* was a collection of poems by various authors, published by Richard Tottel.   23. Sir Thomas   24. variegated pink and white

And in some perfumes is there more delight,
Than in the breath that from my mistress reeks.
I love to hear her speak, yet well I know,
That music hath a far more pleasing sound:
I grant I never saw a goddess go,
My mistress when she walks treads on the ground.
  And yet by heaven I think my love as rare,
  As any she belied with false compare.

This could be nothing other than a parody. Shakespeare assumes a mocking naivety in which he says his lady has none of the wonderful qualities common to the ladies of other poets and yet he thinks her as good as any woman about whom such lies are invented.

An attempt has been made to find a particular sonnet with this dart sticking in it, the favourite being sonnet VII of Watson's[25] *Passionate Centurie of Love:*

Hark you that list to hear what saint I serve:
Her yellow locks exceed the beaten gold;
Her sparkling eyes in heaven a place deserve;
Her forehead high and fair of comely mould;
  Her words are music all of silver sound;
  Her wit so sharp as like can scarce be found;
Each eyebrow hangs like Iris in the skies;
Her eagle's nose is straight of stately frame;
On either cheek a rose and lily lies;
Her breath is sweet perfume, or holly flame;
  Her lips more red than any coral stone;
  Her neck more white, than aged swans yet moan;
Her breast transparent is, like crystal rock;
Her fingers long, fit for Apollo's lute;
Her slipper such as Momus dare not mock;
Her virtues all so great as make me mute:
  What other parts she hath I need not say,
  Whose face alone is cause of my decay.

Although Shakespeare probably has this in mind, the sonnet is not close enough to qualify as the one and only. . . .

But the point of Shakespeare's sonnet certainly seems to be that his lady is odd in lacking the common characteristics of sonnet ladies. And indeed the many sonnets that have been suggested as the source of this parody is proof that no one is specially aimed at. I shall confine my examples to some of those that, as I hope to show, Shakespeare must certainly have read.

There can be no doubt of Barnabe Barnes' sonnet LXXII, which carries something of the cadence or tune of Shake-

---

25. poet Thomas

speare's, which we might expect in a direct parody. It begins

My mistress' beauty matched with the graces

And includes

Love's goddess, in love's graces she surpasseth:

which may have suggested Shakespeare's goddess. In his sonnet immediately preceding, Barnes says that her 'hairs' (in the plural) are of 'angel's gold'. Although the reference is anything but clear, we also find there that Phoebe and Venus have their couches in her cheeks and they are filled with both lilies and roses. In sonnet XLVIII he says he does not ask for jewels from anywhere in the world, but only from his love, and among the diamonds, pearls and rubies he mentions that

Her hairs no grace of golden wires want.

So here is one very striking and relevant item not in Watson. Sonnet XXXIV has this:

My mistress' eyes, mine heaven's bright sun.

. . . He sometimes assaults one particular sonnet, his more general practice is rather to write with one poet in the foreground and others in the background. . . .

My conclusion is that sonnet 130 has a composite background, perhaps not inconsistent with a *Road to Xanadu*-like composition, and that the greater English sonneteers as well as the lesser must suffer its criticism. If the lesser men had never written, there would remain a large enough bull's-eye for its dart to find a home in. I have not yet proved that Shakespeare had read any of these, but I hope the cumulative evidence of correspondences will carry this conviction, especially as among them are particular instances, by themselves, striking enough to be accepted as proof.

GLOSSARY

accentual-syllabic line: A line of poetry with words chosen to make a regular pattern of accented and unaccented syllables.

allegorical guises: From allegory, a two-level story in which events or characters stand for other, sometimes abstract, elements.

alliteration: The repetition of consonant sounds, such as *p*risoner *p*ent.

ambiguous: Term for words or phrases that can be read two or more ways, allowing the poet to say more than one thing at a time.

analogy or **analogical level:** A direct comparison.

apostrophe: The direct address of an absent or imaginary person or thing as if it were present.

apposition: Equivalent words or phrases set adjacent one another.

assonance: The repetition of vowel sounds, such as d*ea*f h*ea*ven.

bathos: Overly sentimental feelings expressed in trite statements.

caesura: A pause within a line of poetry.

cantabile: Smooth, lyrical music, composed with the counterpoint of contrasting sounds.

casuistry: Subtle reasoning meant to mislead.

coda: A passage or stanza bringing a poem or part of a poem to a close.

conceit: An elaborate, strained comparison.

conventions: Standard practices used by poets.

couplet: A two-line unit appearing at the end of a sonnet, commenting on the previous twelve lines.

decade: A unit of ten sonnets.

demonstrative: A word, such as "that," that refers to another element in the sentence.

diction: An author's choice of words.

end-stop: A pause at the end of a line indicating that the unit of thought also stops.

envoi: A passage or stanza bringing a poem or part of a poem to a close.

epigrammatic couplets: The final pairs of lines that state maxims or summarize poems.

exemplum, exempla (pl.): An example.

figurative: Implied, suggested, or metaphoric.

glossing: Interpretation or translation of a word.

hyperbole: Gross exaggeration.

iambic pentameter: An iambic foot is a two-syllable unit of sound with the accent on the second syllable; pentameter means that there are five sound units, or feet, per line.

image: Word group that forms a picture or sound in the reader's mind.

imperative mood: Grammatical expression that commands or directs, such as Step over the wire.

indicative mood: Grammatical expression that states a fact or asks a question, such as You have ideas or Is Mary here?

irony: Words stating one message, but indicating that the opposite meaning is intended.

literal: Directly stated.

metaphor: An implied comparison.

meter: The regular rhythm of a poem created by ordering the accented syllables.

method: The employment of devices to order a poem.

mode: The poetic method, in this case, of a sonnet.

mood: In grammar, the various forms of verbs available to control the way meaning is taken.

octave: The first unit of eight lines in a sonnet.

parody: An imitation, often humorous.

personification: The poetic device of giving human qualities to nonhuman things.

punning: Wordplay, usually humorous, suggesting multiple meanings of a single word.

quarto: A book with pages folded twice, each leaf making a quarter of a page.

quatrain: A four-line unit in a poem.

rhetoric: The art of using language effectively and persuasively.

rhetorical devices: The various techniques that make style effective.

rhetorical question: A sentence worded as a question, that does not call for an answer because it is intended to suggest an effect.

rhyme scheme: The pattern of rhymes at the ends of lines of poetry, marked with a different letter for each rhyming set, such as *abba.*

sestet: A unit of six lines in a sonnet.

subjunctive mood: Verb forms signaling conditions contrary to fact, such as I demand that he go or If I were you.

synechdoche: A figure of speech in which the part signifies the whole or the whole signifies the part.

syntax: Word order in a sentence.

tenor: The drift of an argument; or, that which is meant in a metaphor.

CHRONOLOGY

1557

Shakespeare's parents, John Shakespeare and Mary Arden, marry

1558

Elizabeth I becomes queen of England

1561

Philosopher and statesman Francis Bacon born; advanced as actual writer of Shakespeare's plays by skeptics in modern age

1562

First English participation in New World slave trade from Africa

1564

William Shakespeare born

English dramatist Christopher Marlowe born

Italian painter, sculptor, and architect Michaelangelo dies at age eighty-eight

1569

John Shakespeare becomes bailiff of Stratford

CA. 1570

Emilia Bassano, daughter of a court musician and suggested real-life dark lady of the Sonnets, born

1572

Ben Jonson, English playwright and poet, born

1576

The Theatre, England's first playhouse, is built in London

1577–1580

Sir Francis Drake's first English voyage around the world

1578

Historian and printer Rafael Holinshed publishes *Chronicles of English History to 1575,* source of material for Shakespeare's histories

1582

Shakespeare marries Anne Hathaway

1583

Daughter Susanna born

1584

Sir Walter Raleigh founds Virginia colony on Roanoke Island

1585

Twins Hamnet and Judith born

1587

Execution of Mary, Queen of Scots, by order of Elizabeth I
Marlowe's *Tamburlaine* performed in London

1587–1590

Shakespeare acting and touring

1588

Spanish Armada defeated by British navy, making way for
  England's ascendancy in world trade and colonization

1591

1 Henry VI

1591–1592

2 and *3 Henry VI*

1592

Robert Greene attacks Shakespeare in print, the first known
  reference to Shakespeare's reputation or work
Galileo proves objects fall at the same rate regardless of
  their weight, in Pisa

1592–1593

The Comedy of Errors
Sonnets
Richard III

1593

Plague in London
Marlowe dies in tavern brawl
Titus Andronicus
The Taming of the Shrew
The Two Gentlemen of Verona

Love's Labour's Lost
Venus and Adonis published

1594

Lord Chamberlain's Men, Shakespeare's acting company, formed
The Rape of Lucrece published

1594–1595

A Midsummer Night's Dream
Romeo and Juliet
Richard II

1595–1596

The Merchant of Venice

1596

Shakespeare applies for and receives coat of arms in his father's name, achieves gentleman status
Hamnet Shakespeare dies
King John

1597

Shakespeare buys New Place, property in Stratford that becomes his family's home
1 Henry IV

1598

The Theatre torn down; timbers used for new Globe
2 Henry IV
Much Ado About Nothing

1599

Globe theater opens
Henry V
As You Like It
Julius Caesar
The Merry Wives of Windsor
"The Passionate Pilgrim" published

1600–1601

Twelfth Night
Hamlet
Troilus and Cressida

1601

John Shakespeare dies
"The Phoenix and the Turtle"

1602

Shakespeare buys land at Stratford
Othello

1603

Bubonic plague strikes London
Elizabeth I dies
James I becomes king of England
English conquest of Ireland
Lord Chamberlain's Men becomes King's Men
All's Well That Ends Well

1604

Measure for Measure

1605

Repression of Catholics and Puritans
Gunpowder Plot to kill James I and members of Parliament
Shakespeare invests in Stratford tithes
World's first newspaper begins publication in Antwerp

1606

Visit by king of Denmark
Ben Jonson's *Volpone*
King Lear
Macbeth

1607

Jamestown, Virginia, founded
Daughter Susanna marries Dr. John Hall

1607–1609

Antony and Cleopatra
Coriolanus
Timon of Athens (unfinished)
Pericles completed

1608

Plague in London
King's Men acquire Blackfriars theater
Granddaughter Elizabeth Hall born
Mary Arden Shakespeare dies

1609

Sonnets and "A Lover's Complaint" published by Thomas
    Thorpe, an edition believed unauthorized
Johannes Kepler proves planetary orbits are elliptical

1610
Cymbeline

1610–1611
The Winter's Tale

1611
The Maydenhead of the first musicke that ever was printed for the Virginalls, first book of keyboard music published in England
The King James Bible published
Shakespeare contributes to highway bill, repairing roads between Stratford and London
The Tempest

1612
Shakespeare's brother Gilbert dies

1612–1613
Henry VIII

1613
The Globe theater burns down
Shakespeare's brother Richard dies
Shakespeare buys house in Blackfriars area
Galileo says Copernicus was right; Vatican arrests him in 1616

1615
Miguel de Cervantes completes *Don Quixote* in Spain

1616
Daughter Judith marries Thomas Quiney
Shakespeare dies

1619
René Descartes establishes modern mathematics (analytic geometry)

1620
Pilgrims establish colony in North America at Plymouth Rock
Francis Bacon publishes *Novum Organum*, insisting that observation and experience are the basis of knowledge

1623
Anne Hathaway Shakespeare dies
Actors Condell and Heminge publish Shakespeare's collected plays in a single volume known as the First Folio

WORKS BY WILLIAM SHAKESPEARE

Editor's note: Many of the dates on this list are approximate. Since manuscripts identified with the date of writing do not exist, scholars have settled on the most accurate dates, either of the writing or of the first production of each play.

1 Henry VI (1591)

2 and *3 Henry VI* (1591–1592)

The Comedy of Errors; Richard III; Sonnets (1592–1593)

Titus Andronicus; The Taming of the Shrew; The Two Gentlemen of Verona; Love's Labour's Lost; Venus and Adonis published (1593)

The Rape of Lucrece published (1594)

A Midsummer Night's Dream; Romeo and Juliet; Richard II (1594–1595)

The Merchant of Venice (1595–1596)

King John (1596)

1 Henry IV (1597)

2 Henry IV; Much Ado About Nothing (1598)

Henry V; As You Like It; Julius Caesar; The Merry Wives of Windsor; "The Passionate Pilgrim" published (1599)

Twelfth Night; Hamlet; Troilus and Cressida (1600–1601)

"The Phoenix and the Turtle" (1601)

Othello (1602)

All's Well That Ends Well (1603)

Measure for Measure (1604)

King Lear; Macbeth (1606)

Antony and Cleopatra; Coriolanus; Timon of Athens (unfinished); *Pericles* completed (1607–1609)

Sonnets and "A Lover's Complaint" first published by Thomas Thorpe (1609)

Cymbeline (1610)

The Winter's Tale (1610–1611)

The Tempest (1611)

Henry VIII (1612–1613)

FOR FURTHER RESEARCH

ABOUT WILLIAM SHAKESPEARE AND HIS POEMS

Peter Alexander, *Shakespeare's Life and Art.* London: James Nisbet, 1939.

Ivor Brown, *How Shakespeare Spent the Day.* New York: Hill and Wang, 1963.

Samuel Taylor Coleridge, *Shakespearean Criticism (1811–1834),* ed. T.M. Raysor. Cambridge, MA: Harvard University Press, 1930.

Hardin Craig and David Berington, *An Introduction to Shakespeare.* Rev. ed. Glenview, IL: Scott, Foresman, 1975.

Edward Dowden, *Shakespeare: A Critical Study of His Mind and Art.* New York: Harper & Brothers, 1880.

Harley Granville-Barker and G.B. Harrison, eds., *A Companion to Shakespeare Studies.* New York: Cambridge University Press, 1934.

Barbara Herrnstein, ed., *Discussion of Shakespeare's Sonnets.* Boston: Heath, 1964.

Edward Hubler, Northrop Frye, Leslie A. Fiedler, Stephen Spender, and R.P. Blackmuir, *The Riddle of Shakespeare's Sonnets.* New York: Basic Books, 1962.

Dennis Kay, *Shakespeare: His Life, Work, and Era.* New York: William Morrow, 1992.

Victor Kiernan, *Shakespeare: Poet and Citizen.* New York: Verso, 1993.

Murray Krieger, *A Window to Criticism: Shakespeare's Sonnets and Modern Poetics.* Princeton, NJ: Princeton University Press, 1964.

Sidney Lee, *A Life of William Shakespeare.* New York: Dover Publications, 1968.

J.B. Leishman, *Themes and Variations in Shakespeare's Sonnets.* London: Hillary House, 1961.

J.W. Lever, *The Elizabethan Love Sonnet*. London: Methuen, 1966.

George R. Price, *Reading Shakespeare's Plays*. Woodbury, NY: Barron's Educational Series, 1962.

F.T. Prince, *William Shakespeare: The Poems*. London: Longmans, Green, 1963.

A.L. Rowse, *Shakespeare the Man*. New York: Harper & Row, 1973.

Samuel Schoenbaum, *William Shakespeare: A Documentary Life*. New York: Oxford University Press in association with Scolar Press, 1975.

Martin Seymour-Smith, *Shakespeare's Sonnets*. New York: Barnes & Noble, 1963.

Edith Sitwell, *A Notebook on William Shakespeare*. Boston: Beacon Press, 1948.

Logan Pearsall Smith, *On Reading Shakespeare*. New York: Harcourt, Brace and Company, 1933.

Theodore Spencer, *Shakespeare and the Nature of Man: Lowell Lectures, 1942*. 2nd ed. London: Collier-Macmillan, 1949.

Caroline F.E. Spurgeon, *Shakespeare's Imagery and What It Tells Us*. 1935. Reprint, New York: Cambridge University Press, 1987.

R.J.C. Wait, *The Background to Shakespeare's Sonnets*. New York: Schocken Books, 1972.

John Dover Wilson, *An Introduction to the Sonnets of Shakespeare for the Use of Historians and Others*. New York: Cambridge University Press, 1964.

ABOUT ELIZABETHAN THEATERS AND TIMES

Joseph Quincy Adams, *Shakespearean Playhouses*. New York: Houghton Mifflin, 1917.

Maurice Ashley, *Great Britain to 1688*. Ann Arbor: University of Michigan Press, 1961.

Arthur Bryant, *Spirit of England*. London: William Collins, 1982.

Elizabeth Burton, *The Pageant of Elizabethan England*. New York: Charles Scribner's Sons, 1958.

John Cannon and Ralph Griffiths, *The Oxford Illustrated History of the British Monarchy.* New York: Oxford University Press, 1988.

Will and Ariel Durant, *The Age of Reason Begins: A History of European Civilization in the Period of Shakespeare, Bacon, Montaigne, Rembrandt, Galileo, and Descartes: 1558–1658.* Vol. 7 of *The Story of Civilization.* New York: Simon and Schuster, 1961.

Alfred Harbage, *Shakespeare's Audience.* New York: Columbia University Press, 1941.

G.B. Harrison, *Elizabethan Plays and Players.* Ann Arbor: University of Michigan Press, 1956.

A.V. Judges, *The Elizabethan Underworld.* New York: Octagon Books, 1965.

Walter Raleigh, ed., *Shakespeare's England.* 2 vols. Oxford: Clarendon Press, 1916.

Shakespeare and the Theatre. London: Members of the Shakespeare Association of London, 1927. (This is a series of papers by a variety of critics.)

E.M.W. Tillyard, *The Elizabethan World Picture.* New York: Random House, n.d.

George Macaulay Trevelyan, *The Age of Shakespeare and the Stuart Period.* Vol. 2 of *Illustrated English Social History.* London: Longmans, Green, 1950.

INDEX